THE 7 PILLARS OF NUMEROLOGY

57 Techniques to Decode How Numbers Like Your **Birthday** Affect Your Life and Destiny. A Beginner's Ultimate Guide to **Spiritual Meaning** of Numbers for Everyday Living

MONIQUE WAGNER

Table of Contents

Introduction

There is so much mystery surrounding the origin of numerology, but the most famous myth suggests that the practice began in Pasargadae, an ancient Persian city. Pasargadae was built by the Greek demigod Perseus and his wife, Andromeda, queen of Ethiopia. Their first son Perses was born in 706 B.C.E. *(The History of Numerology, 2022)*. When he turned six, he began complaining about his name. Perses' parents did not take his complaints seriously until a stranger heard the boy muttering along the palace grounds one day. The stranger, cloaked and dirty, asked if he could speak to the boy's parents. Unconvinced of what such a beggar could do for him, Perses thought he would humor the stranger's request and invited him inside the palace to meet his parents. Upon meeting Perses' parents, the stranger unveiled himself. He was Poseidon, the god of the sea. He claimed that from then on, the boy would be called Kourosh Jahangir Hakhamanesh, or Achaemenes, and he would one day form the Achaemenid dynasty.

The parents accepted the change but laughed at the thought of their overbearing son forming such a strong dynasty. To them, it was impossible. Yet, they did not know that Achaemenes' soul, body, and personality were numerically reprogrammed according to his new name.

Achaemenes became intelligent and charismatic. He was thoughtful in his words and wise in his world philosophy. His body changed, and he grew a handsome face and muscular physique. Perseus was astounded and awed by his son's change of character, making his 10-year-old son co-ruler of Pasargadae. Achaemenes did not disappoint. He was a great leader. He gave inspiring speeches and found ways to make and keep his people wealthy, happy, and well-fed. He gave his people freedom of speech and religion. At age 16, Achaemenes was crowned king of Pasargadae *(The History of Numerology, 2022).*

Rumors of Achaemenes' kindness spread throughout the world. Various kingdoms longed to join him, feel his protection, and witness his greatness. Thousands of people also aspired to lead the same lifestyle he offered.

With his growing dynasty, Achaemenes met again with Poseidon. Astounded by the changes within him, Achaemenes asked Poseidon what spells he had cast to help him obtain such greatness and so many loving followers. Poseidon then shared a sacred secret with Achaemenes—the secret of numerology.

Everything in the universe has a vibrational frequency. This resonance of certain numbers with our vibrational patterns is then studied by numerology.

Numerology can help you find meaning and direction. It can help you understand your past and reflect on why your path in life has been complex. And through numerology, you can look ahead and change your future.

We all have a destiny dictated by vibration patterns. These vibration patterns coincide with the vibrations of the numbers zero to nine. Once you know what number coincides with your particular vibrations and what this number means, you can change it. When you change your personal, unique set of numbers, you change your vibrations and your future.

After Achaemenes, other great leaders came into power, all equipped to use numerology to control their lives and the fates of those around them. In 549 B.C.E., a king called Darius rose to power. He formed the largest empire in the world, stretching over 35 countries from Egypt to China. Then in 520, he renamed his kingdom and changed the vibrations surrounding his empire's destiny *(The History of Numerology, 2022)*. His kingdom became one of the most innovative, wealthy, and peaceful empires the world had ever seen. Seeing the benefits of numerology for himself, he chose to share the sacred secret with his empire and educated thousands of people.

As the years went on, Poseidon watched the growth of these cities with love and adoration. However, not all the gods felt this way. In 380 B.C.E., a god intending to end the human race visited Darius. He convinced him the Achaemenid Empire would grow if he changed his name *(The History of Numerology, 2022)*.

The god showed Darius a sequence of numbers far more complex than Darius could understand. Trusting the god, he chose to change his name, and less than a year later, Alexander of Macedonia invaded and overthrew the Achaemenid Empire. During the invasion, temples and universities were destroyed, and the numerology books they housed were lost.

Survivors of the once-great empire fled to India, where they became known as Parsis. Today, they have tales of numerology that would captivate even the biggest skeptics. And although they no longer have access to the expanded details of numerology, they have enough wisdom to change a life.

Numerology looks into the connections between numbers and the cosmos, shedding insight into our journeys. Ergo, everything in life has an essence of predictability. The rain on your head and the chance to meet the love of your life are all events you can control. You were destined to be here and have an impactful purpose: you are not a spontaneous cosmic creation. This is your journey, and it is full of potential.

Life has many challenges. Numerology can guide your understanding of these challenges and your expectations in life. But if you are still unconvinced that numbers mean anything at all besides the value they hold, there is one thing that this book can offer you: hope.

I will admit, when I first started learning about numerology, I thought, "Really? How can I foresee my life before it is even started? Why would a higher power even allow this? If he did allow this, how could I possibly understand the meaning of any of it? All this must be a sham. Every calculated answer is simply a vague suggestion of something a million people could go through." I might have been doubtful at first, but it did not take long before I came to believe in the potency of numerology. Perhaps it is true; then again, perhaps not. However, it would seem that one can create the reality that one chooses, particularly in numbers.

In my early years, I was desperately seeking answers to understand the suffering I had endured. At the time, I was reading about numerology in the hope that it could give me some explanation. I did not find the answers I wanted, not in the beginning anyway, because I was not yet a believer. But as I continued to read about numerology, I gained ideas and hope for my future. My chart told me I should be doing something creative, traveling, and helping people. These were not things I had thought of before, but the more I looked into these ideas, the more that I consider them. I was unaware I had been passing up on opportunities that could have made a difference. Unbeknownst to me, there are opportunities out there that could have been a game-changer.

As I grappled with the implications of all this, it slowly dawned on me that numerology had provided me with numerous possibilities for the future; it had been an invaluable source of inspiration. From there, I left my previous job where my hard work and dedication went unappreciated and unrecognized— no more toiling away in obscurity. Instead, I looked forward to other opportunities that are personally stimulating and motivating. And with these realizations, I felt like I had been given a new lease on life. In the following weeks, I was astounded by how content I was while undertaking activities I never expected to do. This had nothing to do with my faith in numerology but the pure joy of doing something new.

I believe that numerology is designed to help you, similar to how it had helped me, and through this book, I'd like to share with you what I've learned about this practice. You will find 57 techniques, tips, and strategies on how the numbers in your life can help guide you to success, decode the spiritual meaning of each number, and reveal how they influence your life and destiny. These techniques, tips, and strategies are peppered throughout the entire book. And it's intentionally designed this way to serve as your guide along each step of the process.

This book will guide you through the pillars of numerology and explain how they shape your understanding and interpretation of numbers. You will find the science behind the theories and practical advice that you can readily apply to your life and relationships. In these pages, you will find a vivid history of the ancient past merged with whimsical ideas and mathematical sequences.

Moreover, as we dive into the power of numerology, you will learn to interpret numbers, create charts, understand the meaning of your given name and birth date, and discover the vibrations that impact your relationships and decisions. The first pillar will cover the fundamentals, while subsequent chapters will focus on teaching different theories and techniques to get incredible results. Know about powerful vibrations that can shape the energy of your relationships. By employing different theories and techniques in each chapter taught in this book, you can sharpen your intuition, understand the motivations of others, and increase your confidence in making important life decisions.

You will likely see incredible results in better understanding yourself and those around you.

With the help of this book, you'll learn how to tap into your inner power, get in touch with your higher self, discover your divine purpose, and put yourself on the pathway of spiritual awakening. It has the information you need to get started.

Our lives are often full of stress and adversity, something I know all too well, as I once suffered from terrible burnout myself. As an empath that came from a Scandinavian background with neo-pagan roots, I have learned how to face these struggles without relying on medication. In my devotion to understanding alternative healing practices, I have collected knowledge from both metaphysical methods and occult traditions. Sharing the expertise gained over a lifetime of experience is now my way of helping those who are in need of healing.

Numerology can guide you with any difficulties or decisions you may face. The answers are already within your grasp. Begin your spiritual journey with this book and let its teachings help you find them.

Pillar 1:
Fundamentals

Chapter 1:
Origins

Pythagoras

Do you remember learning about triangles in your high school mathematics class? If so, you will recognize the name, Pythagoras. You would have spent hours analyzing triangles and trying to allocate their measurements to letters using a formula known as the Pythagorean theorem. Perhaps at the time, you thought there was no need to measure the angles of triangles. What purpose did this mathematical formula have in your everyday life?

In fact, triangles and Pythagoras have great importance in our lives. One spiritual meaning that a triangle symbolizes is the three intricately linked systems of the past, present, and future. In the practice of numerology, understanding these systems give us insights into the reasons behind our behaviors and identities, show us how to become something entirely different if we choose to, and why we may decide against it.

But how did Pythagoras discover numerology? Where did his concept of using the triangle to understand our lives originate? We can muse over the myth that gods and goddesses were the primary providers of numerology, but how true is it? Is there more to the story?

Pythagoras believed that there was more to life than simple coincidental existence. He believed that, with the precision of the universe, coincidence could not exist. And that every single thing on this earth had an underlying purpose. Nothing was existential, and everything that played out is part of destiny.

According to ancient sources, Pythagoras was born in 570 B.C.E. to a well-off family of merchants in Samos, Greece *(Joanna, 2022)*. His father was a jewel carver, and his mother was a native of Samos island. Pythagoras lived in a well-educated and creative family setting. Throughout his life, even in early childhood, Pythagoras traveled extensively. He spent much time in Egypt, where he learned from various philosophers, religious people, and great leaders. Pythagoras devoted his life to pursuing knowledge, fascinated by possibility and reality. This fascination is a driving force behind his life that he supported with philosophy and mathematics. The tale of the Achaemenid Empire also influenced Pythagoras, prompting him to develop an entirely novel approach to numerology. However, his system was never created with humans in mind. Instead, it was designed to analyze patterns of the universe and the Earth's constant changes due to the interference of the cosmos. Pushing the boundaries of knowledge and understanding, Pythagoras endeavored to gain insight into the behaviors and dispositions of Earth. His systems had a sole focus, not to study humanity's reason for existing but to predict and comprehend our environment more accurately.

It was speculated that around 480 B.C.E., Pythagoras and his followers fled to Metapontum following persecution *(Blakeley, 2022)*. It was unclear how he died, but following his death, his work was seized and hidden due to its politically threatening content. Even so, this did not stop renowned philosophers from referring to his teachings in an attempt to escalate their ideas.

Plato and Aristotle

A Greek philosopher called Plato started the first academy, where he used many of Pythagoras' teachings within the scholarly content. Similarly, Aristotle used Pythagoras' ideas on numerology, metaphysics, and math to better understand the universe and the earth as a geocentric model, a center-lying planet in a constantly moving universe.

More students converted to the Pythagorean way of life and attempted to share his work with the world. Their ravings created a power conflict between Pagans, Catholics, and Christians. The ruling Christian church believed that the practices of numerology, astrology, and divination were forms of magic and proof of the devil's existence. As a result, they destroyed numerology books, schools, and teachings.

The Middle Ages

Building on the ideas of Pythagoras, belief in destiny was a powerful concept during the Middle Ages, and numerology was seen as a way of deciphering its secrets. And despite the many decades that have gone by since then, numerology has managed to stay relevant and continue to stand the test of time.

In the years since its destruction, Pythagoras' teachings moved to Byzantium and formed a large portion of the growing Islamic faith. Those educated in numerology, or Kabbalah, were held in high regard because they housed the knowledge of destiny, divination, and how to change one's life course. Kabbalists were like Pythagoreans because they believed that all life was a manifestation of the numbers one to nine and that each letter of the Hebrew alphabet corresponded to a number *(Abbot, 2021)*. Therefore, every letter in a person's name and every number associated with their life has significance. This significance is in the form of a vibration which matches a specific trait or experience. By determining this likeness, one can understand who they are and their reason for existing.

Numerology became heartily accepted by magicians, occultists, and even some religious leaders during the Middle Ages.

The First Mother of Numerology

In 1847, Mrs. L. Dow Balliett was born. She was a student of both the Bible and Pythagoras *(Drayer, 2003)*. Accordingly, she took it upon herself to add further depth and understanding to the Westernized approach to numerology. As alluded to by Pythagoras, each number between one and nine has an intrinsic vibration or tone, much like musical notes, that form the building blocks of life itself. Throughout her life, she worked to enlighten people and help them improve their lives by making choices associated with their number systems. Her system became known as the Balliett system.

The Second Mother of Numerology

Mrs. L. Dow Balliett was renowned for her work and teaching many philosophers who adopted and developed her ideas. At the young age of 14, Dr. Juno Jordan had the privilege of studying under Mrs. Balliett, with whom she went on to modernize numerology. Her innovative work made it clear that numbers have souls and attribute akin to humans, ultimately bringing this branch of science to life in the Western world.

Dr. Juno Jordan and Mrs. L. Dow Balliett were two of the most influential figures in the history of numerology. Their contributions to the field were connected in several ways.

Numerology Today

Numerology has been modernized to fit our more contemporary lifestyle. We live in a different time than those before us, one in which we possess individual traits and destinies that are uniquely ours. Pythagoras believed in reincarnation, suggesting that we have repeatedly returned to fulfill the same purpose. In this current life, however, we have new goals that only we can achieve in our lifetime. Together, these experiences allow us to embrace our destiny like never before so we may shape a unique and tangible purpose for ourselves.

Discovering who you are in this life, your connection with the divine, and learning lessons from previous experiences can help pave the way to changing your destiny and finding your purpose. By understanding the larger picture, you can take charge of your life and create a future that aligns with your visions.

Chapter 2: Science

Perhaps, you are curious about finding proof beyond mere tales and uncertain accounts.

Numerology is not an exact science but draws from scientific theories and beliefs. At its core, the concept proposes that everything in the universe has a numerical value, a personality, and a purpose. Though scientists may be unable to use statistical evidence to support numerology's predictions, descriptive data from those who have used the practice are a testament to its power and potential. Faith in the spiritual connection between all things is at the heart of numerology's philosophy.

From how much money is in our bank accounts to the number of children we have, numbers touch all aspects of life. Our finances can dictate where we live and how much we spend when shopping. Additionally, the hours worked contribute to our income and the state of our relationships. Even something seemingly inconsequential as our birth date, impacts us since it correlates with astrological signs that can affect personality. All in all, we constantly interact with numbers, and they help shape the scope of our lives.

In life, our names conceal a number that defines who we are and our purpose. Yet, if fate has already decided the course of our lives, where does free will come in? It may be hard to believe that something as simple as numbers can have such an immense impact on us. Whereas if everything is predetermined, how can we make any changes?

According to some numerologists, life is just like a game of Monopoly. We are born after consulting with our advisors and deciding the timing and location of our birth. Our characters, residences, potential allies, and enemies are all chosen in advance. Ultimately, we determine who we might team up with or leave behind. But once the game has kicked off, it is up to us to choose when we invest in a property, embark on an adventure, or decide if we would rather shell out cash to be set free or take our chances with a get-out-of-jail-free card. When the game is over, we must move beyond simply passing "Go." That is how things are. But arriving there involves a mixture of predetermined elements and decisions that are up to us.

Numerology cannot tell you what small choices you will make; it would not anticipate if you will do something clumsy or turn down an opportunity. Nonetheless, it can give you insights into where you belong, your true self, and your dreams for life. Grasping your identity and understanding the why behind it can be incredibly liberating. And acceptance of that is an even greater power, unlocking many doors. Once you know where you are supposed to be, you can get there quickly. However, life without numerology is like playing Monopoly without knowing the rules. Navigating through it can be disorienting, even maddening. It may seem like you are just going around in circles and wasting time. But with knowledge of numerology, you can take action and make decisions that are meaningful, well-reasoned, and part of a larger design.

How It Works

Numerology is the practice of assigning numerical values to letters in order to analyze and understand the meaning behind a person's name or birthdate. Each letter of the alphabet is assigned a numerical value, and these values are added together to create a single digit number that represents a person's personality traits, life path, and more.

To calculate a person's name number, the numerical values of the letters in their name are added together and reduced to a single digit. For example, if someone's name is John Smith, their name number would be calculated by adding together the values of each letter in their name: J (1) + O (6) + H (8) + N (5) + S (1) + M (4) + I (1) + T (2) + H (8) = 36. Then, 3 + 6 = 9. Therefore, John Smith's name number is 9.

To calculate a person's birthdate number, their birthdate is broken down into individual digits and added together. For example, if someone was born on July 3, 1990, their birthdate number would be calculated as follows: 7 + 3 + 1 + 9 + 9 + 0 = 29. Then, 2 + 9 = 11. If the number is a master number, such as 11 or 22, it is not reduced further.

Numerology also involves the use of personal year cycles, which are calculated by adding the individual digits of a person's birthdate and the current year. For example, if someone was born on August 1, 1990 and the current year is 2022, their personal year cycle for 2022 would be calculated as follows: 8 + 1 + 2 + 0 + 2 + 2 = 15. Then, 1 + 5 = 6. Therefore, the person's personal year cycle for 2022 is 6.

Numerologists have created formulas for calculating the value of specific dates, events, and ideas. The theory suggests all numbers can be reduced to a single digit between one and nine. While the calculations themselves may be simple, the interpretation of these numbers requires knowledge and expertise.

Numbers Have Personalities

All numbers have specific properties, traits, genders, and meanings. A double-digit number containing two of the same digits is known as a "master number." Master numbers evoke spiritual powers in their owners. Numbers can be good, evil, masculine, feminine, light, or dark. They exist in the same space and have some differences. Look at them like a newborn baby who likely receives traits from both parents. Even an adopted child will share some characteristics with their caretakers. It was not possible to live for 20 years with someone and not take on similar ideas and attributes as theirs. Hence, numbers, inventions, thoughts, and ideas all have as much energy and potential for meaning as we do.

Meanwhile, the names of people, places, businesses, and countries can be transformed into numerical values, regardless of how many letters are in the alphabet or what language is used to speak. For example: "C" is three in English, while "B", "西", and "bh" are all three when spoken in Hungarian, Chinese, or Zulu, respectively *(Learn Languages, 2019)*. From that, it makes it possible to analyze these names without language-related barriers.

Likewise, birthdays and birth names are the most critical factors in predicting your destiny. Your life path number is the result of breaking down your date of birth into its last value. Furthermore, your soul, personality, maturity, and karmic numbers can be calculated from a similar equation, which we will discuss later.

Chapter 3:
Experiences

Kimberly

Kimberly lived a particularly unlucky life until she discovered numerology. She was lonely, had no money, no friends, and could not keep a job. After graduating from university, her father passed away. With her mother ill and unable to provide financial support, Kimberly was left with no choice in her career path. Out of gratitude for having a job, she accepted what came her way; however, three years of being unappreciated had worn her down and made her realize she needed to find something to make her happy.

One day while browsing the internet, she discovered a numerology forum and paid for a reading that changed her life forever. Desperately seeking something to believe in, she immersed herself in practice. After scrutinizing her number, she realized that certain scenarios were not coincidences. Her observations showed that when her numbers interacted with the environment, the results were destined to occur.

After exploring numerology, Kimberly uncovered a guide to her true self. This allowed her to discover the skills she possessed, what truly inspired her, and where she was headed in life. Once she knew, she made decisions to enable her to move forward toward her destiny.

She took part in and passed a course in software design. Her final results were outstanding and led to dozens of companies outsourcing her for her ideas and ethics. With her head held high, she attended several interviews over short months. While attending the interviews, she fell in love with the owner of a software company. The two were married a short while later and now have two sons. Both are extremely happy, confident, and passionate about their lives. It was all possible because of the growth she managed with numerology.

Taylor

Taylor was disappointed that her life was not going as she had envisioned. She felt lost and miserable in every aspect of her life, from work to home. Uselessly searching for something that could make her genuinely happy, she realized only emptiness would follow. Her days were mundane and foreseeable—a feeling she could not bear. Yet, when a friend visited one weekend, Taylor's perspective shifted when they discovered numerology. After calculating their numbers together, it seemed as if Taylor could truly understand herself from a deeper level than ever before.

Each of her traits, ideas, and experiences was there. The same occurred for her friend. Both had calculated profiles that matched who they were eerily. After the visit, Taylor borrowed her friend's books and started reading further into the practice. Taylor discovered that she was not suited to a repetitive environment but was meant to travel and dabble in the arts. She had always wanted to explore the world but never thought she could. Numerology pushed her toward following her dreams and artistic endeavors. It woke her up and helped her discover who she was.

The world tells us things, and our friends and family can sometimes instill something we are not. When we repeatedly tell ourselves this something, it eventually becomes an unshakeable truth in our minds. We can start to feel that what we have been saying to ourselves is true, even when it is not. Once we begin thinking a certain thought, it can become difficult to convince ourselves otherwise. But there is always that part of us that says, *"Is this really what I want? Is this really who I am?"* And that tiny part complains day and night, telling us we are unhappy. We get so used to being sad that we think it is a part of us. How often have you told yourself, *"That is how it is."*? Yet, these are lies. Life is not supposed to be too hard. Some people are happy and love their lives; you can be like them.

With numerology, you may discover your true self. It brings to mind our childhood aspirations and reminds us of who we once were. Through the practice of numerology, we can recall our hopes and dreams for the future.

Emma

At age five, Emma dreamt of performing like Bruce Springsteen as a dancer, actress, and role model for children. She would invite youngsters into a room and sing them her heart out, though it yielded few results. The kids were not interested in her festivities. It made her happy to try anyhow. But, as she grew older, the world told her that having a small audience was silly. Her voice was all right, but the dancing was a no-go. Unfortunately, strutting your stuff and constantly moving around on stage did not fit the idea of being "ladylike."

Struggling with ADHD and autism, she cocooned herself within a shell of protection. She strove to make her small teaching business thrive. Practicing humility, she never patted herself on the back despite her accomplishments. Eventually, her business made a hefty profit allowing her to buy a fantastic house and meet an incredible guy who could see through all the masks she had built up until then. He would ask her, *"Why do not you sing for me? Why do not you play the piano anymore?"* Her response was often a shrug and an excuse: *"No one wants to hear me play. It is too much effort for no reward."* But deep inside, she knew that was merely a lie; she had been deceiving herself for years.

One day, a student came to her lesson and left behind a book. She picked it up and read the title, *"Numerology."* Emma browsed through every page and worked through every calculation in the book.

For Emma, it was like she was looking into a mirror painted with numbers. Gazing at her numbers, she realized she was destined to be an icon. But living in a bustling and affluent city, it seemed that no one could recognize her true identity. The numbers she embraced were at odds with those around her, and nothing could change that. It was clear that happiness would remain out of grasp for her there.

Before, Emma had always wanted to leave the city, but she had never been able to think of a valid reason to. Besides, who would like to move out of a big city where you make lots of money? However, as soon as she realized who she was, she knew what had to be done. She told her husband that her dream was to become a singer and could not be achieved in the city. Without hesitation, he got into the car, and they headed out to start anew in a small town in England.

Emma's destiny was to find herself cornered and then to find the courage to leave. It was her life's plan. She never knew that until she discovered numerology. Today, she has signed with a small record label in the

UK and performs regularly at private events. She and her husband are happier than ever, and it is because of numerology.

Everyone's journey is unique and special; there must have been a reason you were brought into this world. This book can guide you on your quest to discover the true purpose of your existence. No matter who you are, you belong in this world. Trust yourself and find out what destiny has in store for you.

Pillar 2: Systems

Chapter 4:
The Pythagorean Approach

Ever wondered what the future holds? Unlock your power to know everything about yourself and others with numerology. Create a chart and gain insight into what lies ahead. With this capability at your fingertips, you are capable of so much.

To become an expert in numerology and use its power, you first need to understand how to draw a chart. Start by drawing a triangle upside-down, then cut it into thirds horizontally. Next, you should draw a vertical line that cuts through the top two spaces, then two more vertical lines in each of the top boxes. In the end, your inverted pyramid should have seven sections. This inverted pyramid represents your Pythagorean numerology chart. In this chart, you will calculate your character and destiny *(Richard, 2020).*

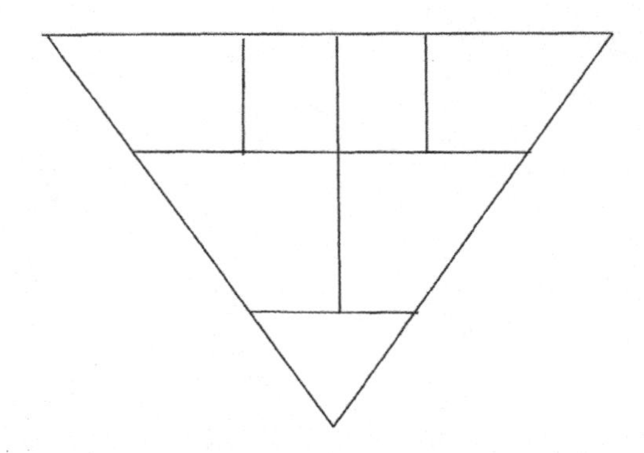

Root Number

Now that you have your chart, you need to calculate your Pythagorean numbers. Begin by noting your date of birth in the order of the day, month, and year. Make sure to write this value on the topmost point of the triangle.

For example, Michelle LaVaughn Robinson Obama was born on the 17th of January, 1964 *(Michelle Obama Biography, 2018)*. This is how that date should be written:

17, 01, 1964

First, add her birthday digits and reduce them to their most basic value between one and nine.

1 + 7 = 8

Subsequently, write the number eight in the top far-left corner of your triangle. Following this, add her birth month numbers and reduce them. You can write this number to the right of her birthday number.

0 + 1 = 1

To start, the two digits of her birth year must be added and reduced. The outcome can then be written in the third box on the top row.

Repeat this same procedure with the last two digits of her birth year, writing down the answer at the far-right corner of the top row.

1 + 9 = 10 = 1 + 0 = 1
6 + 4 = 10 = 1 + 0 = 1

The top of your triangle should read as follows:

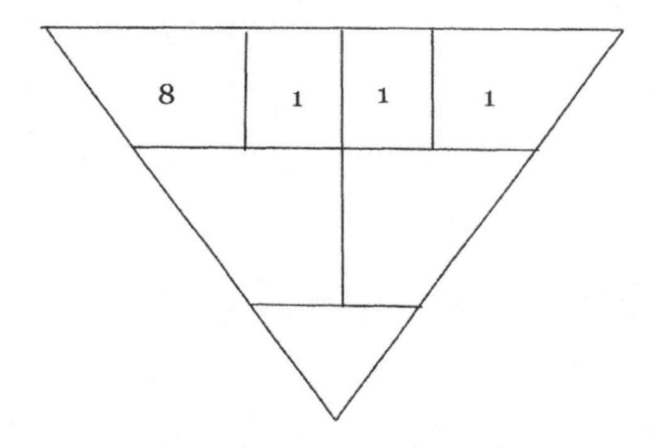

To reduce the right and left numbers, add eight and one together, then write the reduced number in the position below. Likewise, do the same for the other numerical values on the right.

8 + 1 = 9 and,
1 + 1 = 2

The second line of your triangle should read as follows:

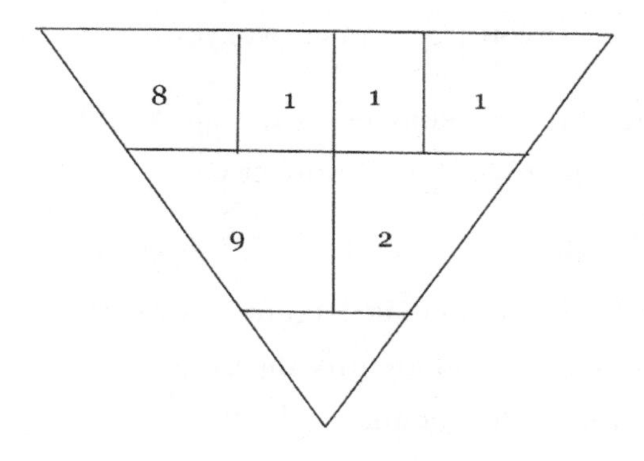

Lastly, you must add the two central digits and reduce them. You can write this value at the bottom of your triangle.

9 + 2 = 11 = 1 + 1 = 2

Your triangle should read as follows:

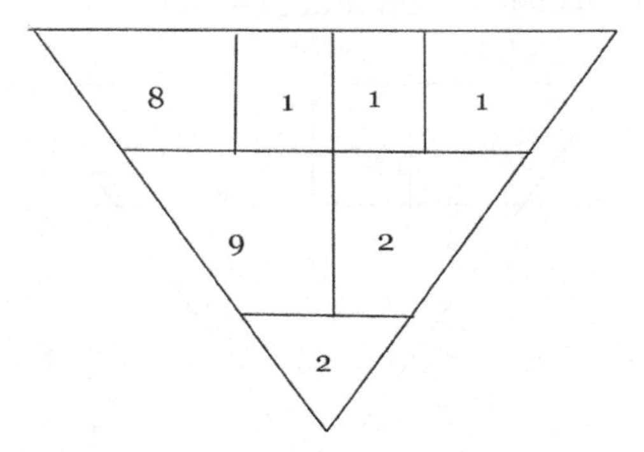

The last number you obtain is your root number. It plays a vital role in determining your destiny, the opportunities that come to you, and the obstacles you face. Moreover, it uncovers your unique identity and character. Thus, its impact on shaping our future is significant.

In numerology, the number two is a supreme feminine force. I do not know Michelle Obama personally, but that description sums up her media presence well. This number represents grace and power, peace and balance, and cooperation. The number two is one of the most intrinsically feeling numbers. If you are number two, you connect well with others.

Michelle Obama's numerology chart has already demonstrated truthfulness, which many people can connect with.

Have you ever wanted to learn how to calculate your external characteristics based on a triangular diagram? Look at Taylor Swift's birth chart for further insight and identify the numbers along the sides of the triangle. Let us dig in deeper and explore!

Taylor Swift was born on the 13th of December, 1989 *(Taylor Swift Biography, n.d.)*. We will begin by writing her birthday at the top of the triangle to ensure we make everything right.

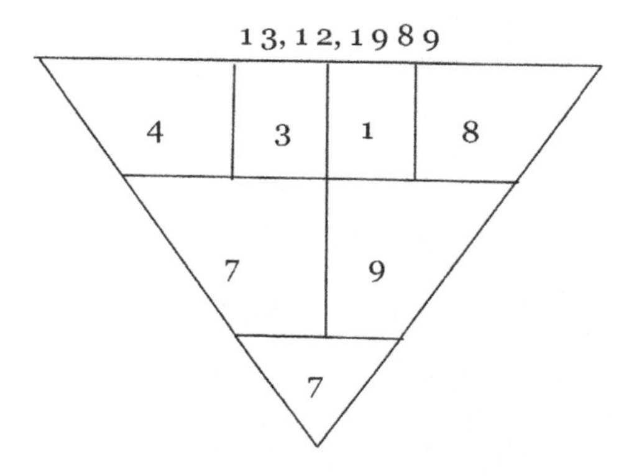

From here, we can go about calculating Taylor's root number. Add the numbers associated with her birthday and place them in the first space on the left:

$$1 + 3 = 4$$

After that, enter the digits associated with her birth month and write them in the second space:

$$1 + 2 = 3$$

Afterward, fill in the third slot using the first two digits of her birth year:

$$1 + 9 = 10 = 1 + 0 = 1$$

Lastly, you should add the last two digits and write them in the last space on the far right:

$$8 + 9 = 17 = 1 + 7 = 8$$

Add the value of the two left and right fields and write it in the field below. Then add these two fields together so that you end up with a final digit at the very bottom.

4 + 3 = 7
1 + 8 = 9
7 + 9 = 16 = 1 + 6 = 7

Taylor Swift has a root value of seven.

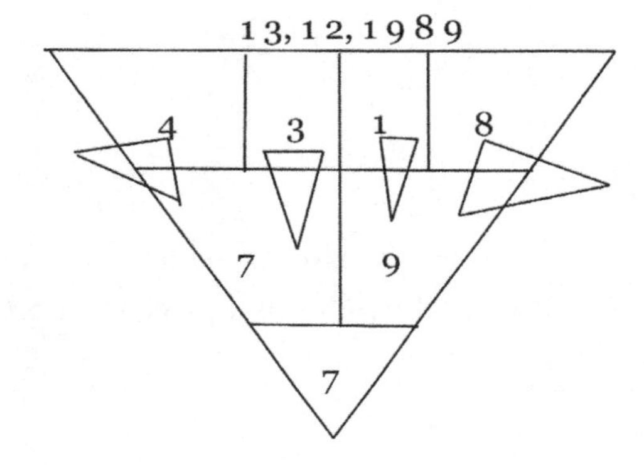

Now that you have determined Taylor's root number, envision mini upside-down triangles joining the numbers from the top row to those in the middle. First, take the number in the upper-left corner and sum it up with the one to its middle-left number:

4 + 7 = 11 = 1 + 1 = 2

Do the same process on the right side:

9 + 8 = 17 = 1+ 7 = 8

The next step is to take the number from the second box from the left and add it to the one in the middle-left section:

3 + 7 = 10 = 1 + 0 = 1

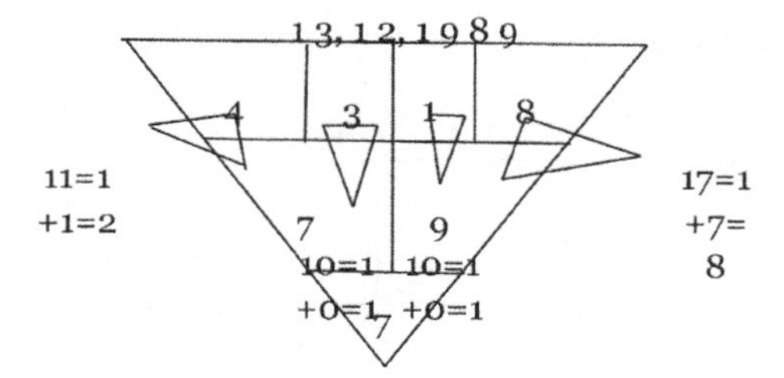

After that, carry out the same process on the right side:

1 + 9 = 10 = 1 + 0 = 1

When you have your numbers, add the ones on the left-hand side and reduce them to their simplest form. The same goes for the right-hand side, reducing them to their most basic value.

2 + 1 = 3 on the left and 8 + 1 = 9 on the right.

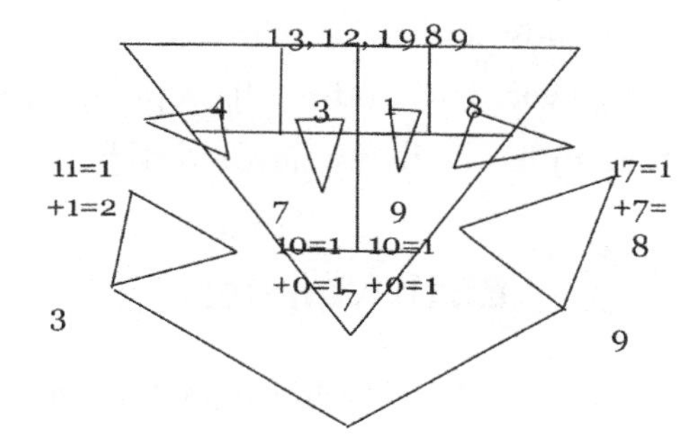

Finally, add these two numbers and reduce the result to its most basic form.

3 + 9 = 12 = 1 + 2 = 3

Taylor Swift has an expectancy number of three.

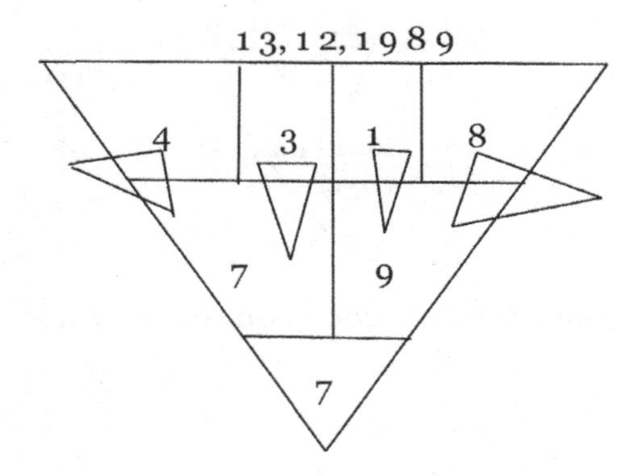

This number symbolizes who you are to others and what they expect from you. A number three is a vibrant, engaging, and amusing number that jumps joyfully and enthusiastically connects with other people. This number is so exhilarating that it has the potential to draw together romantic partners, friends, and those with the same interests. Judging from the behavior of Swift fans and media representations, the world views Taylor Swift as an iconic figure devoted to her music and fans.

Birth Number

The talents and potential that you hold can be uncovered with the help of your birth number. This number is so easy to figure out. All you need to do is add the digits corresponding to the day you were born. Having this number can help you to reach your destiny, as it encompasses the pieces of you that are essential for you to get there.

Let us take a look at Vincent van Gogh's birth chart. He was born on the 30th of March, 1853 *(Biography of Vincent van Gogh, 2009)*. The day of his birth is the 30th. To calculate his birth number, we will add these two values and reduce them to a root value:

$3 + 0 = 3$

The number three in numerology is often associated with creativity, self-expression, and the power of manifestation. It embodies enthusiasm, optimism, and the ability to communicate and express ideas. The number three resonates with the energies of the ascended masters and is considered the number of divine manifestation. Looking at Vincent's extraordinary flair for artistic expression, his innovative techniques, and his fervor for life, one might speculate if the vibrational energies of the number three influenced his journey. While there's no certainty that he was aware of his numerological significance, the universe, in its mysterious ways, often aligns numbers and destinies in synchronicity.

First Impression Number

Your first impression number is the number on the left in the middle row of your upside-down triangle. If you still remember, you can find this number by adding your day and month of birth together. Let us look at Ted Bundy's birth chart. He was born on November 24th, 1946 *(Lopez, 2021).*

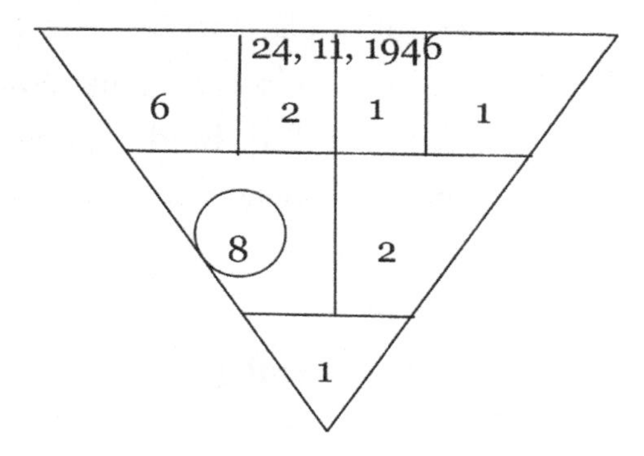

The number eight on the left is Bundy's first impression and portrays them in a successful light. With a keen eye for business and a Karmic sense, eight will pay back whatever he put into the universe. This number also speaks of how they see themselves and interact with the world. Ted Bundy believed that what he was doing was okay. For years, he was able to portray a "perfect boyfriend" image due to his charming looks. After his capture, Ted even took on his case for many trials. During this time, he played the role of a successful, balanced individual with perfect Karmic reasons for doing what he had done.

If his parents knew numerology, could they have stopped him? Could they have put a stop to the atrocities before they even began? Nowhere on any numerology scale does it say your career path will be a murderer, a singer, the wife of a president, or an artist. Our lives are predetermined to a certain extent, but the rest is free choice. Ted Bundy was destined to be a businessman, an independent, intellectual force. He was always going to do something charismatic. But Ted chose to be a killer even though he could have become the greatest president the world has ever known.

There is no way of knowing what decisions you will make. Yet, understanding yourself and how you relate to others can help you avoid destructive and hazardous scenarios, enabling you to live the life of your dreams. For such, numerology can give you insight which is somehow similar to you keeping away from a place because you know the potential destruction that the area can face. However, numerology would not provide you with specifics, like your little brother potentially being the one to cause the destruction. These details are beyond its capabilities, at least in Pythagorean numerology.

Soul Number

This number reveals your heart's greatest desires, the things you have always wanted, and the path that will lead you to your ultimate happiness. To calculate this number, you will need to find the numerical value of each vowel in your full name. Then, add them together and reduce that final number to its ultimate value between one and nine.

For instance, my name is Monique Wagner. The vowels in my name are O, I, U, E, A, and E. So, in Pythagorean numerology, every letter in the Latin alphabet is assigned a number from one to nine. To get the numerical value of each letter, count from one through nine and repeat the sequence:

1	2	3	4	5	6	7	8	9
A	B	C	D	E	F	G	H	I
J	K	L	M	N	O	P	Q	R
S	T	U	V	W	X	Y	Z	

Hence,

O = 6
I = 9
U = 3
E = 5
A = 1
E = 5

Let us put these together and discover my soul number:

$$6 + 9 + 3 + 5 + 1 + 5 = 29 = 2 + 9 = 11 = 1 + 1 = 2$$

Being an individual with a soul number two, I am fulfilled when connecting and helping others. And I am astounded by how accurately this mirrors me. Socializing and interacting with others also brings joy to me, as does making new friends and discovering different perspectives on life. From that, the sole purpose of this book is to help people find their way in life and connect with them on a deeper level. *What is your soul number? Does it accurately reflect who you are and what your true passions are?*

Character Number

People often look at your character number as an indicator of who you are and how you will be perceived. It is like a first impression, determined by the values of all the consonants in your name. Adding up the consonants and reducing them to their simplest form gives you your character number.

Let us use jazz singer Nina Simone's name in this example.

In February 1923, Eunice Kathleen Waymon was born (Nina Simone, n.d.) and later became an icon of the burgeoning Western jazz scene. Taking on the stage name Nina Simone, she flourished as a musician; only her friends knew her as Eunice. But in her daily life, *who was Eunice Kathleen Waymon to others? And who was she as Nina Simone?*

Eunice Kathleen Waymon has the consonants N, C, K, T, H, L, N, W, Y, and M. Now, let us use the chart to calculate the worth of each letter.

Thus,

N = *5*
C = *3*
K = *2*
T = *2*
H = *8*
L = *3*
N = *5*
W = *5*
Y = *7*
M = *4*
N = *5*

Then,

$5 + 3 + 2 + 2 + 8 + 3 + 5 + 5 + 7 + 4 + 5 = 49 = 4 + 9 = 13 = 1 + 3 = 4$

As Eunice, she was rigid and decisive in all matters of morality, had a steadfast dedication to her work, and was not one to be diverted by the luxuries of life. She approached every task with great seriousness and commitment yet remained exceptionally composed and structured.

Considering if Nina Simone was different while performing, let us look at her name. While looking at the name of iconic artist Nina Simone, we see five consonants: N-N-S-M-N.

Accordingly,

$N = 5$
$N = 5$
$S = 1$
$M = 4$
$N = 5$

Lastly,

$5 + 5 + 1 + 4 + 5 = 20 = 2 + 0 = 2$

On stage, Nina Simone was a beacon of feminine power and beauty. She cared about her fans and wanted to have a connection with them. Her voice was not just an instrument of sound but a bridge that could bring together people, races, and communities.

When Nina took on a stage name, she modified how people viewed her and her destiny. Who she was on the stage was only sometimes who she was at home. By doing this, she allowed herself to be open to other individuals.

Expression Number

Uncovering your expression number can be an insightful experience. It reveals the talents, strengths, and abilities that are already inside of you. Knowing the value of each letter in your name, adding them together, and then reducing them to their most basic form is how this figure is achieved.

Now, let us embrace the knowledge and learn more about it by looking at a fictional character, Winnie the Pooh. We will see the uncanny parallel nature of Pythagorean numerology to characters invented by us.

Using the alphabet chart on the previous page, we will let it guide us.

$P = 7$
$O = 6$
$O = 6$
$H = 8$

Then,

$$7 + 6 + 6 + 8 = 27 + 2 + 7 = 9$$

Nine is characterized by completeness, unity, compassion, and usefulness. It yearns to spread joy and lend a helping hand to others. This number is perfect, holy, and spiritual and supports Karma. Reminiscent of Winnie-the-Pooh's values, nine stands for all these qualities.

Chapter 5:
Chaldean Methodology

The Chaldean numerology system is believed to have originated in ancient Babylon, around 4,000 years ago. The Chaldeans were a group of people who lived in southern Mesopotamia, in what is now modern-day Iraq. They were known for their advanced knowledge of astronomy, mathematics, and other sciences, and were instrumental in the development of the Babylonian civilization.

Their system is based on the vibrations and energies of the numbers 1 through 8, which are associated with specific letters of the alphabet. The Chaldeans used this system to predict the future, make important decisions, and gain insight into the personalities and characteristics of individuals.

Over time, the Chaldean numerology system spread throughout the Middle East and Asia, where it was used by various cultures and civilizations. It was later introduced to the Western world by the Greek mathematician Pythagoras, who is also credited with developing the Pythagorean numerology system.

This is how an Ancient Chaldean alphabet chart would be assigned numerical values *(The Surprising Ways, 2022)*:

1	2	3	4	5	6	7	8
A	B	C	D	E	U	O	F
I	K	G	M	H	V	Z	
J	R	L	T	N	W		
Q		S		P			
Y				X			

The Chaldean number system assigns them based on the sound when the letter is spoken (also called its vibration), instead of the position it has in the alphabet.

Today, Chaldean numerology is still widely used by practitioners and individuals seeking spiritual insight and guidance. Its unique approach to numerology, which takes into account the energies and vibrations of individual letters, sets it apart from other numerology systems and makes it a valuable tool for personal growth and self-awareness.

First, Second, and Third Names

Your first name can often give clues about your interests and habits. Then, your middle name holds your soul's energy, talents, and heartfelt desires. The last name may suggest how our friends and family influence us. Each element of your name carries a unique value linked to you and your destiny *(The Surprising Ways, 2022)*.

Let's take the example of the full name "Michael Jordan" to demonstrate how to calculate and interpret the Chaldean numerology value:

M = 4
I = 1

C = 3
H = 5
A = 1
E = 5
L = 3

J = 1
O = 7
R = 2
D = 4
A = 1
N = 5

Adding these values together gives us:

4 + 1 + 3 + 5 + 1 + 5 + 3 = 22 (Master number)
1 + 7 + 2 + 4 + 1 + 5 = 20 (Reduced to 2)

Therefore, the Chaldean numerology value of the full name "Michael Jordan" is 22/2 (depending on whether or not we reduce the master number).

According to Chaldean numerology, individuals with a name number of 22 are believed to be powerful manifestors and visionaries who can achieve great things on a global scale. They are often natural leaders with a deep desire to make a positive impact in the world. Individuals with a name number of 2 are seen as intuitive and diplomatic, with a strong desire for harmony and balance in their relationships; characteristics that Michael Jordan exude.

The Rearranged Birth Number

The Chaldean system focuses specifically on the day of birth rather than on the month and year *(The Surprising Ways, 2022)*. Now, let us look at Albert Einstein's birth number in this example.

Einstein was born on the 14th of March, 1879 *(Albert Einstein Biography, n.d.)*. The significant number here is 14, which can be reduced to 5. Both numbers 14 and 5 give us an accurate reading of Einstein's destiny and character. In fact, having the number 14 can bring luck in finances. Those blessed with this figure can expect wealth and riches to follow.

Based on that, Albert Einstein was a German theoretical physicist who had accumulated $65,000 by the end of his life. Today, that money is worth $634,000 *(Albert Einstein Net Worth, n.d.)*. To compare that, the average American between 60 to 70 years of age has about $266,000 *(Wang, 2022)*. Einstein had almost three times that. He was not Elon Musk with $222 billion, but he was better off than most *(Jin & Oguh, 2022)*.

Meanwhile, number five suggests that Einstein was a creative man who loved to travel. By analyzing Einstein's travel diaries, one can see that he was a man who traveled a lot and enjoyed doing so. He was also known as a creative genius. From there, without a doubt, the Chaldean method of numerology is one of the most detailed and accurate systems to use. However, there may be limitations to its usage.

Chapter 6: Kabbalah Numerology

It was believed that before the beginning of time, God gave ancient knowledge to the angels. This ancient knowledge was known as the Kabbalah. The angels first delivered it to Adam, the first man. When God told Adam and Eve to leave the Garden of Eden, Archangel Raziel gave Adam a second chance. This second chance allowed him to acknowledge his reason for existing. With the knowledge of his strengths and weaknesses, God empowered Adam to craft a competent and instinctive race. However, they became more intrigued by what the Earth had to offer and how they could benefit from it than by the ways of the Lord.

Around 1700 B.C.E., Archangel Melchizedek gifted Abraham with the Kabbalah *(Slick, 2008)*. With this ancient knowledge, Abraham spoke with God and made a covenant with Him. God asked Abraham to find the Hebrew people. In return, God promised to make the Hebrews and Abraham great and blessed peoples. As promised, the Hebrews became a great nation. Meanwhile, Abraham had the power of the Kabbalah and God on his side when he fulfilled his covenant with

Him. Unfortunately, after Abraham's descendants were enslaved in Egypt, the Kabbalah was again lost.

Finally, years later, Moses went to Mount Sinai to meet God and receive the Ten Commandments. God gifted Moses with the Kabbalah. This time, God had placed the Kabbalah in the right hands. Moses protected the Kabbalah and its teachings but paid the price for it. Many of Moses' followers who participated in Kabbalah practices were persecuted and tortured. Due to that, the Kabbalah was practiced and taught through whispers in the dark. The practice was originally a male oral tradition and later changed to incorporate a wide range of people *(Slick, 2008)*.

According to the writings, Rabbi Akiva discovered the first book containing Kabbalah teachings in a cave believed to be God-given. To make these teachings accessible to more people, he rewrote them into a work called the *Sepher Yetzirah*. Centuries later, Moses de León wrote another book based on scrolls purportedly belonging to Abraham. He reinterpreted and rearranged the original practice into an alternative interpretation *(Slick, 2008)*.

For centuries, books have explored Hebrew Kabbalah numerology with the help of mathematicians, philosophers, and religious leaders. This practice encourages us to "receive" to consider our true meanings, strengths, and weaknesses, how to improve ourselves, and our purpose on earth. By doing so, we can live a more fulfilling and joyful life.

Kabbalah Energies

Kabbalah numerology places great importance on the names of people and living things rather than their numerical value alone. By decoding the value of someone's birth name, they can unlock their future, solve existing challenges and even prevent them from occurring. Understanding Kabbalah Numerology involves ten distinct energies: Kether,

Chokhmah, Binah, Chesed, Geburah, Tiphareth, Netzach, Hod, Yesod, and Malkuth. These energies are best represented in a Tree of Life diagram, which reveals insights into the true nature of each energy type.

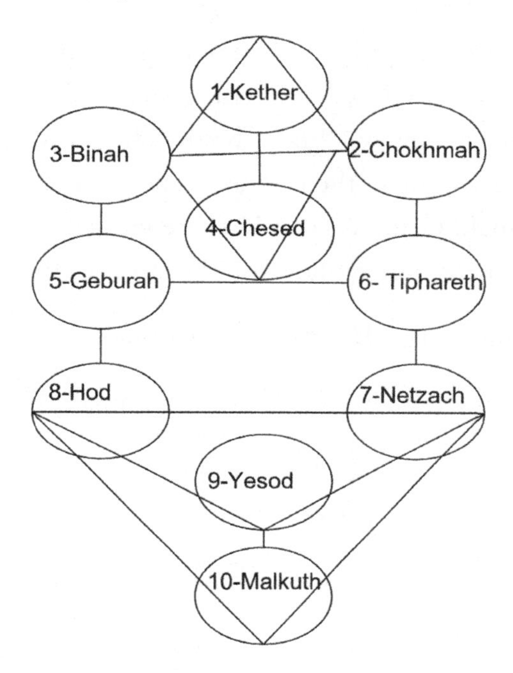

Each of the ten energies is associated with a numerical value *(Kabbalah Numerology, n.d.)*:

Kether = 1

Chokhmah = 2

Binah = 3

Chesed = 4

Geburah = 5

Tiphareth = 6

Netzach = 7

Hod = 8

Yesod = 9

Malkuth = 10 = 1 + 0 = 1

Knowing where your energy is in comparison to other energies is essential. Location can provide insight into the collective and individual effects of the energy and its related energies on a person.

Along the center lies a spiritual divinity focused on interpersonal conflict and wholeness. Kether, Tiphareth, Yesod, and Malkuth represent it. In the right column, we find Chokhmah, Chesed, and Netzach, energies centered around their actions and how they affect others. Meanwhile, Binah, Geburah, and Hod are located in the left column; these energies focus more on how other people see them.

Everyone's destiny is shaped by these energies *(Kabbalah Numerology, n.d.)*:

- The energy Kether is linked to Chokhmah, Binah, Yesod, and Malkuth *(1, 2, 3, 9, 10)*.
- Chokhmah has ties to Kether, Binah, and Chesed *(2, 1, 3, 4)*.
- Binah is connected to Chokhmah and Geburah *(3, 2, 1, 5)*.
- Chesed is linked to Binah, Geburah, Tiphareth, and Netzach *(4, 3, 5, 6, 7)*.
- Geburah has ties to Binah, Chesed, Tiphareth, and Hod *(5, 3, 4, 6, 8)*.
- Tiphareth is linked to Chesed, Geburah, Netzach, and Hod *(6, 4, 5, 7, 8)*.
- Netzach is connected to Chesed, Tiphareth, Hod, Yesod, and Malkuth *(7, 4, 6, 8, 9, 1)*.
- Hod has ties to Geburah, Tiphareth, Netzach, Yesod, and Malkuth *(8, 5, 6, 7, 9, 1)*.
- Yesod is linked to Netzach, Hod, and Malkuth *(9, 7, 8, 1)*.

Kabbalah Alphabet

The Kabbalah numerology alphabet chart is the same as the Pythagorean chart, allocating each letter in the Latin alphabet to a number within the repeated sequence of one to nine *(Kabbalah Numerology, n.d.)*:

1	2	3	4	5	6	7	8	9
A	B	C	D	E	F	G	H	I
J	K	L	M	N	O	P	Q	R
S	T	U	V	W	X	Y	Z	

Your Ultimate Kabbalah Number

To uncover your ultimate Kabbalah number, all the letters in your full name must be associated with their corresponding figures. Add them together, divide the sum by nine, and take the remainder plus one to arrive at the number *(Kabbalah Numerology, n.d.)*.

For example, Amy Winehouse. Born on September 14th, 1983, Amy Jade Winehouse was a gifted British singer whose blues and pop tracks like *"Rehab"* and *"Back to Black"* quickly captured the hearts of many.

The values associated with the letters of her name can be noted as follows:

A = 1
M = 4
Y = 7
J = 1
A = 1
D = 4
E = 5
W = 5

I = 9
N = 5
E = 5
H = 8
O = 6
U = 3
S = 1
E = 5

So,

Amy Jade Winehouse = 1 + 4 + 7 + 1 + 1 + 4 + 5 + 5 + 9 + 5 + 5 + 8 + 6 + 3 + 1 + 5 = 70
70 divided by 9 = 7.77

After the decimal, the remaining value is seven.

7 + 1 = 8

Amy Winehouse had a Kabbalah value of eight, which stands for recklessness. From the moment of her birth, she was destined to live a life of glory, beauty, and creation, thanks to the energy of Hod connecting Tiphareth, Netzach, and Yesod. This destiny seemed all too clear, considering she was notorious for taking drugs, having turbulent relationships, and frequently being in challenging situations. Incontestably, anyone who has seen her perform or attentively listened to her music would confirm this. Her openness was demonstrated through live shows, studio sessions, and even on the streets with the paparazzi. Likewise, Amy achieved great success; she won awards, and her music received widespread acclaim. Fans admired her, and the production agencies adored her. But most of all, she was a creator; just like magicians put on their suits, she pulled songs out of thin air. However, Amy was undoubtedly a risk-taker to achieve all that she had. And with a lifetime value of eight, it is obvious she would frequently get involved in precarious situations.

Pillar 3: Numbers

Chapter 7:
Pythagorean

Below is a detailed list of the meaning of each of the most basic numbers in the universe, how they apply to your personality, and what they imply about your destiny *(Number Meanings 1–9, 2022)*.

- ### *One*

  The number one is a natural-born leader, eager to invent new things and pave the way for others. It is as inspiring as it is motivated, pushing others to fulfill their wildest goals and ambitions. Proactive and independent, it needs no permission to be creative, ambitious, and innovative. Movement and momentum surround this pioneer; its goal-oriented attitude can be both a force and a beacon of creativity. Although powerful, the number one can also be manipulative, doubtful, uninhibited, self-centered, and reckless.

  Becoming an executive, entrepreneur, contractor, manager, law enforcement officer, lawyer, engineer, sailor, producer, writer, designer, or inventor may be the paths many take. Notable persons with life path number one include Martin Luther King Jr., Bill Gates, Steve Jobs, and Mother Teresa. Others like Lady Gaga, Kate Winslet, and Gwyneth Paltrow have followed this same pattern.

- *Two*

Number two is characterized as a supremely empathetic and feminine power, which stands for gratitude and strength. Those under its influence are generally cooperative, giving, respectful, and balanced. As a peacemaker with an intuitive spirit, this number can forge partnerships to make it even more powerful. It also has a greater ability to connect and communicate on a deep soul level. Then, its mediation skills help it see things from different perspectives in any given situation. This number is also influential, unifying, discreet, supportive, protective, and inclusive, but it can be indecisive due to its many options. Likewise, it may be unassertive or apprehensive about stepping up as a leader when needed and can easily be hurt by others.

People with a destiny value of two are often drawn to jobs that allow them to make an impact in the lives of others, from teaching and counseling to architecture, law, and medical science. Caregiving and beauty are also popular professions for those with destiny number two. Prominent figures with this same destiny value are Madonna, Jennifer Aniston, Diana Ross, Jennifer Lopez, Kanye West, and Jackie Kennedy.

- *Three*

Number three brings positive vibes, enthusiasm, and vibrant energy. Life is always exciting when you are with someone who is a three. They have an exuberant youthfulness and optimism that is contagious. Being around them is daring and friendly, they make friends quickly as they love talking to people, recognizing their unique qualities, and learning from them. This zest for life makes them communicative, artistic, charming, curious, and ever-optimistic. Yet, threes can also be naive, unfocused, and shallow. Hard times never appeal to them, as threes like to be in situations that allow their joyful personalities to shine through.

Creative minds with a life path number three often find themselves in careers such as artistry, writing, production, speaking, design, journalism, politics, law, philosophy, psychology, and counseling. Public relations managers and athletes are also known to be part of the group. Some people with a life path number three include David Bowie, Christina Aguilera, Hillary Clinton, John Travolta, Jamie Foxx, and Shania Twain.

- *Four*

Individuals who bear the number four are no-nonsense folks in their approach to life. Pragmatic, levelheaded thinkers are also dependable, steady, and conservative. Rather than attempting to be inventive, they take part in tried-and-trusted practices of how things operate. The four's wise energy assists them in providing reasonable explanations, with everything being seen as black or white and nothing in between. These practical people are loyal and willing to help, although they may come across as rigid, unbending, dogmatic, and hard-lined.

Ideal career fields for four are financial planning, economics, managerial sciences, engineering, law, software design, architecture, landscaping, mechanics, and banking. Some fours you might know are Drake, Nicki Minaj, Oprah Winfrey, Brad Pitt, Jimmy Fallon, Usher, and Elton John.

- *Five*

Those born under the number five are endlessly curious, pushing themselves to explore new experiences and lead adventurous lives. With a big-picture outlook, they try to make the best out of any situation. As for their adaptability, nothing fazes them. This number is ready for anything. Despite their flexibility and determination, fives could have some negative traits, such as being untrustworthy, inconsistent, or directionless. But these people would not let that stop them from living life to its fullest.

People who identify as fives often thrive in professions like art, writing, acting, design, travel, photography, public relations, negotiation, law, sailing, architecture, flight attending, management, and stunt work. They also include some of the world's most renowned personalities, including Vincent van Gogh, Steven Spielberg, and Angelina Jolie; famous singers such as Beyoncé, Jon Bon Jovi, and Mick Jagger.

- *Six*

The number six cherishes its ability to give and receive love more than anything else. It stands for nurturing, lending support, unconditional understanding, and tenderness. Partnerships are where the number six truly shines when it is a close emotional bond. Empathy helps those around them drop their guard and welcome love into their lives. They are excellent parents as well as gentle teachers. Sixes tend to be supportive, protective, intuitive, romantic, and compassionate but can also be idealistic, self-sacrificing, and overly sensitive.

Sixes often work as entrepreneurs, musicians, designers, diplomats, lawyers, coaches, contractors, doctors, teachers, athletes, and chefs. People with sixes include Jessica Alba, Michael Caine, Michael Jackson, and Francis Ford Coppola.

- *Seven*

Sevens seeks to uncover the truth, believing everything is significant and holds a purpose. They are intellectual but also have an intuition cultivated by their constant search for answers. In-depth information is required to satisfy their curiosity and needs to be settled with a shallow explanation. Not only are sevens persistent questioners, often probing into deeper spiritual realms, but they can also be reclusive and guarded due to their skepticism, secrecy, and harshness.

Someone who identifies with the number seven is often in occupations such as counseling, law, medicine, education, designing, writing, freelancing, photography, science, research, or philosophy. Famous sevens you may recognize include Paula Abdul, Muhammad Ali, Kristen Bell, Queen Elizabeth, and Princess Diana.

- *Eight*

This digit is the ultimate achiever and measures success by the goals it accomplishes and the awards it earns. The number eight is lucky, ambitious, and enduring. However, it can also be materialistic, authoritative, and entitled. At the same time, it is balanced and treats Karma respectfully, positioning itself as a friend. With all these attributes, number eight has excellent power to succeed.

Careers for eight are often in entrepreneurship, photography, journalism, law, accounting, architecture, pharmaceuticals, research, and real estate. From Hollywood to the business world, people with life path eight include Sandra Bullock, Penélope Cruz, Martha Stewart, Amy Schumer, and Jessica Simpson.

- *Nine*

The most complete, balanced, and spiritual digit is nine. With this in mind, number nine strives to understand the greater purpose behind all events in life. Performing good deeds brings a sense of joy and happiness while they are also kind, compassionate, and devoted to helping others. Even though it sometimes endures hardship, these moments are captured within to bring about positivity elsewhere ultimately. Number nine is tolerant, patient, supportive, wise, accepting, and kindhearted. Nevertheless, it can be resentful or even overly sacrificial.

Nines are typically sociologists, psychologists, lawyers, designers, diplomats, politicians, researchers, and teachers. Some people with nine life paths includes Jim Carrey, Morgan Freeman, Bob Marley, Prince Charles, Andrew Lloyd Webber, Mozart, Houdini, and Prince.

Chapter 8:
Chaldean

In Chaldean numerology, your root number and compound number are definitive in understanding who you are and what you can expect from your life. Below you will find a long list of symbols and meanings attached to numbers one through 50 *(Olivia, 2022)*.

- *One*

  The number one signifies power, strong leadership skills, and passion. It is highly ambitious and motivated with an inspiring influence. Yet, it can also be associated with dictatorship due to its overbearing and strict nature.

- *Two*

  People associated with this number are well regarded for their cooperative and communicative nature, balanced by a sense of harmony. They tend to form stable connections with others but can be vulnerable to being taken advantage of due to their selflessness. Those born under this numeral are emotionally intelligent, compassionate, and able to work well as part of a team.

- *Three*

Those possessing the number three are renowned for their willingness to lead and guide others and their creative and vibrant spirit. Unfortunately, this can lead to an impulsive way of life and irrational behavior, often resulting in burnout.

- *Four*

Folks tied to the number four are reasoned, independent, and securely grounded. They are welcome during complex scenarios as they carefully process incidents and handle strain well. Though faithfully reliable, they can be obstinate and have little interest in taking risks. Generally preferring stability, they do not care for modifications.

- *Five*

The five elements of earth, water, wind, fire, and spirit are represented by this number. People with this number adapt to change quickly and go with the flow of life, often understanding that everything has a larger purpose. They are usually flexible and multitalented and can naturally adapt to any situation. However, people with this number may need help to focus and become skilled in many activities or none.

- *Six*

Six is a gentle figure, representing tranquility, and is often seen in the natural world. Those who identify with this numerical value are peacemakers gifted with the ability to observe all aspects of a problem. They have wisdom that comes from experience, allowing them to provide wise counsel. Despite their insight, they may find difficulty in actively resolving issues due to a nature that avoids confrontation.

- *Seven*

Individuals with the number seven tend to be introspective and spiritual. Associated with inner wisdom, solitude, and search for truth, they are typically curious about mysticism and are always believing that there is a deeper truth within everything they encounter.

- *Eight*

Represented by the infinity symbol and the concept of eternal life, number 8 means balance and harmony. People associated with this number are encouraged to strive for excellence while finding a healthy balance between the material and spiritual aspects of life.

- *Nine*

This digit represents a sense of humanitarianism, empathy, and selflessness. People with this number are compassionate and generous that stems from the desire to serve others. They favor creativity and emotions above everything else. They lean away from logic and passionately follow their hearts. Yet, they often grapple with tunnel vision and can lose sight of what is most important. ***Ten***

Anyone with the number 10 can achieve much success and honor. These people are usually lucky and have a loyal group of friends.

- *Eleven*

  This number represents intuition, inspiration, and enlightenment. It also represents creativity, self-expression, and individuality. Those with this number may have a heightened sense of intuition and spiritual awareness, and may be drawn to spiritual practices and pursuits.

- *Twelve*

  This number is associated with harmony, balance, and partnership because it represents a blending of the energies of the numbers 1 and 2. Those with this number may have a natural ability to bring people together and create a sense of unity and cooperation.

- *Thirteen*

  Having this number has no bearing on luck. Instead, it is associated with transformation and change. This number represents a period of transition and may indicate a time of upheaval or challenge. However, it also represents the potential for growth and evolution, and they may emerge from this period stronger and more resilient than before.

- *Fourteen*

  This number favors financial well-being above all else. Fourteens are logical, ambitious, and financially aware. They can also be evasive and unreliable, especially when they have to participate in activities they deem unworthy of their time.

- *Fifteen*

  Individuals with this number are generally well regarded. Yet, they can struggle with forming and sustaining relationships when their personality is rigid and unyielding. This attitude may lead to feelings of isolation, bitterness, and exasperation.

- *Sixteen*

  This number is associated with spiritual growth and evolution, and may indicate a time of deepening spiritual awareness and understanding. They may be called to explore their spirituality and to deepen their connection to the divine.

- *Seventeen*

  The power of this lucky number is enduring, spreading its blessings across loved ones and acquaintances alike.

- *Eighteen*

  This number represents a time of transformation and spiritual awakening. It is associated with spiritual rebirth and may indicate a period of spiritual growth and transformation.

- *Nineteen*

  The number 19 is associated with completion and endings and may indicate the end of a cycle or the completion of a project or goal. They may be called to let go of what no longer serves them and to embrace new beginnings and opportunities.

- *Twenty*

People with this numerical identity may be called to pursue further education or to deepen their understanding of a particular subject or area of interest. 20 represents a time of learning and growth and is related to education and knowledge. 20s are more likely to be asked to share their expertise with others and to use their skills and talents to make a positive impact in the world.

- *Twenty-one*

Life for this number is filled with creativity and self-expression. They could explore their artistic side and use their talent to create something meaningful and beautiful.

- *Twenty-two*

Twenty twos are about balance and harmony as well as power and leadership. They can use their influence to create positive change in the world.

- *Twenty-three*

These angelic helping hands of the universe come without expectations. Regardless of the circumstance, they are always available to assist others. They put aside their wants and needs without grappling with their repercussions. Instead, they lead a life empowered by the happiness of others.

- *Twenty-four*

This number enjoys a strong bond with family and friends, who offer unwavering love and emotional support. Lucky in affection, this digit is also blessed with many trusted relationships filled with warmth and understanding.

- *Twenty-five*

Hard-working individuals are represented by this number. Seeing their future clearly and prepared to give everything they have, they always strive once they reach their goals.

- *Twenty-six*

Those with this number are inherently compassionate and devoted to relationships. Despite this, they often find themselves in complicated situations due to their tendency to enter into relationships without thought. Fortunately, resilience is a trait that serves them well in these moments. However, too many missteps can lead to an overload of stress on their shoulders which could cause them to become distrustful, unfaithful, and aggressive.

- *Twenty-seven*

People blessed with the number 27 are knowledgeable and guided by sound logic. As long as they trust in their brilliance, these people will find great success and power.

- *Twenty-eight*

Those with this number are practical and efficient. Their responsibilities and duties are important to them, and they always strive to find a balance between their work and personal life.

- *Twenty-nine*

Having this particular number means that you could find yourself in complex and risky scenarios. Those with these digits tend to be highly trusting and naive, a mix that can make for dangerous situations.

- *Thirty*

Love and affection are likely to be found in this number.

- *Thirty-one*

Number 31 represents artistic talent, inspiration, and success. People with this number should strive for balance between their creative and practical responsibilities.

- *Thirty-two*

This number is also associated with success and prosperity. It could mean that they need to focus on their financial and material well-being.

- *Thirty-three*

Someone with this number is lucky, imparting support and showing love. They are believed to be natural healers and counselors who can inspire others through their example.

- *Thirty-four*

Thirty fours put focus on love and relationships. This could indicate a need for harmony and balance in someone's romantic life.

- *Thirty-five*

Folks numbered 35 are often free thinkers who value their individuality and possess a great deal of creativity. They have a great thirst for knowledge stemming from their desire for personal growth and learning.

- *Thirty-six*

Those with this number are thought to be blessed with luck, power, and optimism.

- *Thirty-seven*

For anyone associated with the number 37, life is filled with luck in relationships, friendships, and finances. A blessed life awaits them, full of joyous companionship.

- *Thirty-eight*

This figure is associated with abundance and success.

- *Thirty-nine*

People possessing this number are usually hardworking. Though they can be stern and unwelcoming at times, they are just as capable of showing joy and appreciation.

- *Forty*

As the digits representing hard work, discipline, and success through effort, people with this number are often ambitious and driven towards their goals. They are driven with achievement, success, and abundance, but may also require balance and self-awareness to avoid neglecting other areas of life.

- *Forty-one*

These people under number 41 have keen instincts. They have a trustworthy gut and should always trust themselves above others.

- *Forty-two*

Individuals born with this number are destined for a life filled with love, support, success, and joy.

- *Forty-three*

The number 43 represents a combination of the energies of the numbers 4 and 3. It signifies success, creativity, and self-expression. Those with this number in their chart are often natural leaders with a practical and grounded approach to life. They have excellent communication skills and trust their intuition to manifest their goals.

- *Forty-four*

People with a strong influence of the number 44 are often highly ambitious and driven, with a natural ability to lead and inspire others. They are known to work hard to achieve their goals and dreams.

- *Forty-five*

Individuals with this number are often successful in their careers and personal lives due to their ability to adapt to changing situations and their determination to overcome obstacles. They have a strong sense of responsibility and a practical approach to life, making them dependable and reliable.

- *Forty-six*

These people are generally very successful in relationships.

- *Forty-seven*

This number is considered auspicious and fortunate. People with this number tend to be natural-born leaders with an ability to inspire others to follow them. They have a strong sense of self and are often self-reliant. They are creative and innovative thinkers who possess the ability to turn their ideas into reality. This number indicates success in all aspects of life, including career, relationships, and personal growth. However, individuals with this number should be careful not to let their ego get in the way of their success. This number can bring negative energy caused by grief.

- *Forty-eight*

The number 48 signifies material success and financial abundance. It is a number associated with leadership, authority, and power. People with this number are often successful in business, finance, and management. They have the ability to make sound decisions and achieve their goals through hard work and determination. They are practical and efficient in their approach, which helps them in achieving their desired results.

- *Forty-nine*

49 people have a strong sense of responsibility and desire to make a positive impact in the world. They symbolize someone who's here to bring spiritual wisdom and knowledge to the world. This number is associated with great leadership abilities, intuition, and a deep understanding of human nature. Individuals with this number are often seen as wise, compassionate, and highly intuitive. They have a natural ability to connect with others on a deeper level and may be drawn to careers in teaching, counseling, or spirituality.

- *Fifty*

It is a combination of the energies and attributes of the numbers 5 and 0. The number 5 symbolizes freedom, versatility, and progress, while the number 0 represents potential, wholeness, and infinity. Together, they create a harmonious blend of energies that signify growth, abundance, and success. Those who are associated with this digits has the potential to achieve great things in life, both materially and spiritually. It is a number of personal transformations and growth, and it may indicate that they're ready to embark on a new journey or chapter in their life. Those influenced by this number are likely to be innovative, resourceful, and confident, and they have the ability to manifest their desires into reality.

Chapter 9: Kabbalah

One cannot simply appeal only to their calculated value. They should also analyze their representative energy, number, and energy collection when identifying their future *(Kabbalah Numerology, n.d.)*.

- *One (Kether or Malkuth)*

  One symbolizes progress, spirit, momentum, and leadership. This digit wants to change the world. Linked intricately to Kether, this digit has a divine connection with the spirit world. People with this digit have a talent for connecting with others and seeing their potential. Kether's ties with Malkuth and Yesod can grant a person skill in speech, art, writing, and music. It believes invention and creativity are the foundation of solving all issues. Likewise, it is connected with Binah on its left, meaning that this digit is also very nurturing and positive. On its right, it is linked with Chokhmah, meaning it is wise, imaginative, and insightful.

- *Two (Chokhmah)*

  Those connected with Chokhmah have an innate sensitivity, feeling things profoundly and having a sharp instinct. Helping others is something they take pleasure in, but their ambition can sometimes overpower them. Twos have ties to Binah, Kether, and Chesed. These energies make them excellent and understanding leaders.

- *Three (Binah)*

  A figure of affection, people linked with Binah are compassionate and wise, bringing understanding, nurturing, and optimism. Further associated with Chokhmah, Kether, and Geburah, this force is disciplined, intuitive, and a brilliant leader, able to resolve issues quickly and confidently while remaining determined.

- *Four (Chesed)*

  This number represents futility and charity. Nothing else matters to these people except helping others. Activities and energy are futile unless they benefit someone. Also linked to Chokhmah, Geburah, and Tiphareth, this energy is nurturing, creative, good at resolving conflict, balanced, and harmonious.

- *Five (Geburah)*

  Five represents newness, innovation, establishment, and travel. These digits can make a home anywhere, find friends in the most unlikely places, and make even the sternest of people kind-hearted. Geburah can set boundaries, be disciplined, and get down to business when resolving a dispute. They are honest and have patience but will always get straight to the point. People with Geburah energy do not back down easily and stand their ground and remain frank no matter what. On top of that, it is closely linked with Tiphareth, Chesed, and Binah, resulting in an equilibrium between harmony, balance, loving-kindness, compassion, and true understanding and wisdom.

- *Six (Tiphareth)*

Symbolizing implementation, strategizing, setting goals, and achieving tasks, people with six built on a foundation of logic and hard labor. Those drawn to Tiphareth strive for harmony and equilibrium, taking what life offers in exchange for what they provide, achieving contentment. Tiphareth also lies in the center of the tree of life. People who associate strongly with this energy get along well with others. They are resilient peacemakers who can think, act, and understand the inner workings of people.

- *Seven (Netzach)*

Those with the number seven are believed to have a magical power that grants them luck. They can remain unshaken and persevere through difficult times while watching out for the safety of others. Connected to Tiphareth and ultimately linked to the Earth, these individuals possess a solid connection to Chesed, Hod, and Yesod, three divine spiritual powers. As such, they can find balance in life and demonstrate great kindness and charity. Their creativity, positivity, and energy make them resilient even when their lives are in danger.

- *Eight (Hod)*

People associated with this number have the power to push through tough times. Nevertheless, their frequent engagement in strenuous scenarios affects their resilience. To stay out of trouble and make the best of the situation, they must be more conscious and stay away from naivety at any cost. The energies of Hod, Yesod, Netzach, Tiphareth, and Geburah converge within them, making them kind-hearted, selfless, balanced, and great at setting limits.

- *Nine (Yesod)*

The luckiest of all symbols is closely connected to Yesod, allowing for a direct connection to the divine. With Yesod being held in harmony with Malkuth, Kether, Netzach, and Hod, this digit carries an innate creativity. It can be relied on for writing, art, and musical excellence while being a fearless leader. Despite any recklessness it may demonstrate, successes will always follow due to its ability to overcome all obstacles.

Chapter 10:
Master Numbers

The values, larger-than-life and double-digit, carry immense power and responsibility. When these numbers are observed, claimed, analyzed, or sensed, the people associated with their presence feel a heightened awareness. These senses may be related to intelligence, intuition, potential, finances, opportunities, or even love. Master numbers include the placement of two like numbers beside each other.

Analyzing these master numbers involves viewing them as they stand and with their reduced value *(Reed, 2020)*. Some master numbers include, but are not limited to:

- ***11***

  Instinctive, influential, and cooperative, the number 11 is often called the Mother of numbers. A feminine energy that is understanding, supportive, and attentive draws people in and can accurately read their energies and intentions. Those with this path are highly perceptive, often serving as seers, clairvoyants, or psychics. However, walking this life path takes work; the strength of their power can lead them to overwhelming dread and a sensation of carrying the weight of the world on their shoulders. This can bring paranoia, depression, fearfulness, distrustfulness, and even unkindness.

- *22*

  People with these digits represent a class of master builders; they are practical visionaries. They can execute all grand ideas with ease through their confidence. Yet, despite helping others achieve their dreams, they remain unfulfilled in life. Always striving for betterment, they seek knowledge and expansion while being ungrateful for what they already have. Success is never enough, as they can never seem to feel its truth, no matter how much it has realized. Thus, these digits signify intense masculinity and logicality, providing a pathway for dreams to become a reality.

- *33*

  This rare number, known as the Master Teacher, has the power to aid and transform people, helping them reach their highest potential. As a result, the person holding this number is destined to show others the path to inner healing and enlightenment, even if they face more pain. Despite constantly searching for themselves, they must accept their plight and act as a positive example by advocating mercy and love. Finding compassion within themselves, trusting their intuition, and forgiving previous mistakes will help them achieve their ultimate destiny.

These individuals possess an extraordinary capacity for expression. From acting to art, singing to scriptwriting, they can impersonate anyone and everyone around them. They are not duplicitous; instead, their creativity skill allows them to appear as someone entirely different. Their calling is to encourage others to develop their capabilities, captivating those in need of assistance. Alas, only a select few of this group can realize their power and utilize it to its fullest potential. Despite its strength, many may never learn to depend on themselves, erase the past, or let love lead the way.

Seeing your master number in everyday life suggests that you are heading in the right direction. When this happens, take a moment to consider what you are thinking and doing, where you are, and what the future holds.

Pillar 4:
Karmic Influence

Chapter 11: What is Karma

Karma is an ancient concept rooted in the Sanskrit word for action *(Believe, 2021)*. It is a Hindu belief that speaks to the cause-and-effect cycle of the universe. When we do something, someone else reacts, influencing our following action. This cycle continues indefinitely since we are all prone to act and have reactions ourselves, even after death. Whatever wrongs or rights you have committed will follow you through this life and even past lives, as the theory of reincarnation suggests. Our actions and mistakes often come back to haunt us; Karma is like divine justice, rewarding us for our good deeds while punishing us for our bad ones.

Life may deal you a great hand of fortune or misfortune. Your attached Karma may be the reason for such. Karma acts like a naughty sibling, always playing tricks on you. It may paint an invisible door in your path and make you believe you have a fantastic opportunity when it does not want that for you. Instead, it shocks you when you realize the door is fake. Likewise, if Karma is happy with you and wishes to reward you, it can align events to ensure you get the opportunities you deserve.

Moreover, what goes around comes around. Your thoughts and energy can affect those around you, so it is best to put out good vibes. Poor choices or negative behavior can come back to haunt you; be mindful of how your actions may affect others. To lead a successful life, try your best to stay positive and act responsibly.

Can you stop or prevent Karma? No, Karma is inevitable. But you can limit its wrath by focusing on living a happy and peaceful life, regardless of the cards you are dealt. In addition, you can calculate your Karmic lessons and debt to help you navigate the challenges that Karma may throw in your path. It can also help you know when to expect good years.

Chapter 12:
Karmic Debt

Throughout our lives, we develop a great deal of wisdom. We can show much kindness and also make many mistakes. Our mistakes need to be corrected. These mistakes accumulate in Karmic debt. To correct our past errors, Karma throws us into situations wherein we are forced to make things right or to live, feel, or behave the way we have moved on others.

Karmic debt is represented by the numbers 13, 14, 16, and 19 *(Believe, 2021).* These numbers may appear to you when interpreting calculations associated with Pythagorean, Chaldean, or Kabbalah numerology approaches. For example, you may attempt to discover your character number but realize your full name is related to the number 14. This is a sign that you have a Karmic debt to pay. Karmic debt numbers work like master numbers. When you discover them, you should analyze the value and the reduced value.

Each of these numbers has a significant meaning which can be interpreted to help you pay for your mistakes in this life and avoid further Karma in the future. Those with these numbers embedded in their numerology chart are likely to have a harder life than others. They are also more likely to be involved in charitable work.

Assigning Debt to Numbers

Below you will find a detailed list explaining each of the Karmic debt numbers, what challenges they evoke, the reasons for their existence in your life, and how you can overcome them *(Believe, 2021)*.

- *13*

  Having a Karmic debt number 13 can be a source of immense frustration. Tasks that should naturally be achievable become arduous and seemingly never-ending, as if there is no end because of the constant interruptions. All this tends to follow from poor decisions, selfishness, and taking advantage of those around you. However, it is necessary to remember that success is not something unattainable. Instead is hard-won through perseverance, even in the most challenging times. The key is not to give up and keep pushing despite adversity. Many successful people have gone through an experience similar to this Karmic debt number 13.

- *14*

  Those with this Karmic debt may struggle to find freedom, becoming trapped in relationships, enslaved by their minds, drugs, companies, or even the whim of nature. As a result of past transgressions and enslavement of others' freedoms, they are required to learn how to master themselves emotionally and be ready for any unexpected twists life might throw at them. The only way out is a dedication to their goals, never giving up no matter what. By maintaining control and staying resilient, they can break free from this Karmic debt.

- *16*

  People with this Karmic debt number are fated to start new projects and be optimistic, only for their dreams to come crashing down around them again and again. All new ventures will never be successful, and every incident will fail. These people will feel a massive ego boost just before the venture fails. When the experience fails, they will find themselves humbled. Likewise, individuals with this number can be very understanding and empathetic. Those with this number must be wary of being selfish and bitter, for that will only stoke the fire. They need to learn to see failure as a blessing and grow more modest as they age. Such a painful price is the result of destroying the faith, belief, and success of others.

- *19*

  Possessing a Karmic debt number 19 comes with many challenges. Independence and power must be used for the greater good, and you must learn to stand your ground and lead others toward freedom. Even those closest to you can hurt and challenge you, making inner peace and forgiveness essential. However, the core lesson of this Karmic debt is the need to ask for help. Not doing so will only bring pain. Ultimately, the cost of such debt is sacrificing your well-being.

Karma might seem like something you cannot escape, but it does not need to be your master. Instead, think of it as a game; Karma has presented you with a challenge and given you the tools to succeed. Sure, you could be angry and ignore the advantages right in front of you. Or you could take the initiative and find more creative ways to progress toward a happy life and reduce any Karmic debt hanging over your head.

Chapter 13:
Karmic Lessons

The choices you have made and the mistakes you have committed in the past can come with a price. This cost is known as "Karmic Debt." Often related to your personal growth and evolution, these lessons may be required for your soul's journey. Such Karmic lessons arise from past actions and thoughts, guiding your path forward. Everything about humanity invokes something to be learned and internalized. How we treat each other reminds us to be kind, courteous, patient, gentle, and cooperative. Mastering these attributes is bound to take time, years, or even a lifetime.

According to some biblical texts, seven archangels, Michael, Raphael, Gabriel, Jophiel, Ariel, Azrael, and Chamuel, deliver messages from God to us humans. As our souls evolve over millennia of life experiences, they learn and gain wisdom that brings them closer to God. Souls who have experienced enough in their journey may become honored as angels. Those who have gone even further and achieved much can receive the greatest honor of becoming archangels and direct messengers of divine power. Guiding us with their wisdom on our path to enlightenment, these unique souls help us progress through our life journeys.

Our Karmic lessons are integral to our spiritual journey, leading us ever closer to God. By learning from these lessons, we become better people, which in turn helps bring peace and strength to those around us. These Karmic lessons can be found by looking at the numbers missing from your full name *(Karmic Numbers, 2020)*. To understand this concept further, let us look at Aileen Wuornos as an example. Born on February 29th, 1956 *(Gomez, 2022)*, Wuornos was a notorious killer who also happened to be a prostitute, robbing and shooting her clients.

1	2	3	4	5	6	7	8	9
A	B	C	D	E	F	G	H	I
J	K	L	M	N	O	P	Q	R
S	T	U	V	W	X	Y	Z	

First, we need to understand what numbers are associated with Aileen's name to establish the ones that are not.

A = 1
I = 9
L = 3
E = 5
E = 5
N = 5
C = 3
A = 1
R = 9
O = 6
L = 3
W = 5
U = 3
O = 6
R = 9

N = 5
O = 6
S = 1

Aileen had a name with the numbers one, three, five, six, and nine; missing were two, seven, and eight. Based on the Karmic lessons of these numbers, she was warned of the potential consequences if she did not heed its advice. Number two cautions against thoughtless action, letting one end up hurting others, while slow steadiness should be employed to enjoy life. Seven suggests carelessness and lack of intuition, often leading to situations that could have been sidestepped with some thoughtfulness. On the other hand, eight implores one not to remain isolated but instead share the love, which is not a sign of weakness despite feeling like it is. In Aileen's case, impulsive behavior combined with reticence indicated that she never learned those Karmic lessons, something evidenced in the events and outcomes of her life.

Assigning Numbers to Lessons

Below, you can find a comprehensive list of numbers and the associated Karmic lessons that may help you discover what life intended for your soul's growth. Not all are obliged to accept these lessons. Some are here to show others the way, some to settle debts, and some just to be here *(Karmic Numbers, 2020).*

- *One*

  A procrastinator of note, this number channels a character who suffers from an abundance of ideas but cannot start any of them. Your thoughts and projects accumulate in your head without being able to put them into action. This leads to frequent self-criticism and low self-esteem, further undermining your efforts. To be truly fulfilled, you must push yourself and find the courage to devise techniques to get going.

- *Two*

Your actions may often be inconsiderate and self-focused, but it is time to sit back and watch how things unfold before jumping in. Reacting too quickly can come at a cost, so sometimes it pays to wait before moving. There could be unforeseen benefits that you had not anticipated.

- *Three*

This number reveals someone who can be too easily hurt by their self-criticism. Constantly putting yourself down and being too hard on yourself will only lead to discouragement. Acknowledge and give credit for your efforts, no matter how small the achievement may be. Appreciating yourself is a must; it will help you move forward and continue striving for greatness.

- *Four*

Feeling aimless and stuck, you may struggle to focus on one thing. Even when you try, it is like trudging through mud. But there are ways to move forward by finding a balance between your professional and personal lives. Learning tactics to concentrate can help you progress and discover a sense of direction again.

- *Five*

Staying within your comfort zone can lead to a life of missed opportunities. It is essential to remember that there is a whole universe out there for you, and it may pass you by if you do not take the initiative. Instead of retreating into isolation, look for an adventure, challenge yourself, and come out of your shell, as this will open up exciting new possibilities.

- *Six*

Working on numerous tasks at once can be overwhelming and challenging to complete. When multiple projects remain unfinished, it is essential to learn to focus on one and cross it off the list before moving on to the next. Finishing something is much more satisfying than having five things in progress.

- *Seven*

Reckless behavior puts your safety and the safety of those around you at risk. Acting without thinking can lead to troubling situations, so it is essential to consider all aspects before acting. Taking the time for thoughtful planning is necessary for success.

- *Eight*

Someone who tends to be proud and independent might find it challenging to ask for help. But learning to do so can bring peace that cannot be seen by struggling alone. Life will inevitably throw battles our way, but rather than facing them as individuals, you should not be afraid to reach out for support. The results will undoubtedly be better than trying to handle everything alone.

- *Nine*

When you talk to others, you have difficulty understanding their perspectives. Being unsure of how to respond or act in certain situations can lead to feeling confused about the behavior of those around you. Following your intuition and being open-minded can help you form better relationships and start engaging with life. Striving to ask questions and gain insight into why people act the way they do is crucial for living a full, meaningful life.

Knowing your Karmic lessons helps in understanding what role you have to play in this life. It gives our suffering and experiences meaning and reminds us that there is more to life than simply existing. Enjoyment and learning go hand in hand. To live a fulfilled life, we need to know where our skills are lacking. When we practice and refine those skills, they become stronger, and life becomes easier.

Furthermore, finishing off the lessons we need to learn in this life puts us in good stead to learn new lessons in future lives. We can open ourselves up to a peaceful existence for years to come, but we have to start now. Take little daily steps to improve yourself, and you will find happiness along the way.

Pillar 5:
Angel Numbers

Have you ever noticed the same digits repeating over and over? It could be the numbers on your clock reading 5:55, 4:44, 3:33, 2:22, 1:11, or even 12:22. Or you were on holiday and found yourself walking up a certain road and seeing the number 777 on every street you crossed. On their own, these numbers are simply coincidences. But when witnessed three or four times in a day, week, or even hour, the numbers can be associated with angelic messages. When you encounter angelic messages, pay attention as something important is happening.

Angel numbers are spiritual messages in numerology that can guide us, confirm our actions, or redirect us to safer paths. People who have a strong intuition and sense of spirituality will notice these messages quickly. Skeptics and disbelievers will need some help receiving and interpreting angelic messages. But although the numbers may be present, some people either do not pay attention to them or do not care.

For such, imagine that you are going to a school concert for your child. As you look for your kid, you spot them happily smiling on stage. Because your focus was on finding your child, you had missed a little preschooler shoving their teacher off the bleachers and into the audience. You would have seen it if you were fully looking at the entire stage. Such is the power of having a broad view and understanding of situations.

So, to truly understand the greater picture, you must be willing to open yourself up to a power larger than you. You must believe someone is seeking your best interests and guiding your life toward a predetermined purpose. This purpose is not simply about raising a family or achieving the perfect job, it is something much bigger. Once you recognize this, you will be presented with more possibilities than ever and an entirely different way of viewing the world.

But why do you see angelic numbers? Why now and not yesterday? Why this year and not three years ago? Everyone develops at their own pace, and the ability to open up to the possibility that life is larger than what it seems takes time. Before we can even imagine how big the world is, certain events need to occur. The events that lead us to believe may be predetermined or happen coincidentally.

Imagine that you are destined to end a relationship of seven years. Suppose the decisive moment is at seven o'clock at a house on the seventh street, yet you do not make it. As a result, you miss your chance for a life-changing event and never progress further in life. On top of everything, it takes another eight years before you make the breakup. Unbeknownst to you, the love of your life has been waiting around the corner during that time. Unfortunately, your shot had already passed because you were not paying attention, leaving you unaware of what could have been yours within just a few months.

Once you spot these numbers, it is almost as if you invited them into your life. You anticipate what knowledge they may bring, and the value of this message can be seen in its ability to save you eight invaluable years. Pay close attention; this could be the key to unlocking something extraordinary.

To open yourself up to angelic messages, you must first be aware of their presence and potential. You can start by analyzing your surroundings and taking in the presence of numerals within them. Look around you now. *Are there any numbers in the space you are in?* Maybe it is an alarm, a watch, a thermometer, a bill, or an account number. You do not need to write these numbers down; you just need to make yourself aware of them. Every day, take some time to look around you and take note of the numbers in your vicinity. Perhaps set the alarm to go off at different intervals throughout your week. When your alarm goes off, look around where you are and take note of what you are doing. Look for numbers in the room and see if they are familiar. At first glance, nothing may appear out of the ordinary, but as time passes, you will sense something like déjà vu. Though the link may not be obvious, it will cause your memories to awaken. But when you feel that touch of déjà vu in your mind, you will know that you are finally open to receiving angelic guidance.

Chapter 14:
The Power of Three

When you first see a series of digits, you should ask yourself if this is a message or a coincidence. The general rule is that seeing a number once is as coincidental as seeing it twice. These are merely numbers within a space. There is still a limited possibility that they mean anything at all—until they appear a third time, you can interpret them as messages *(5 Powerful Ways, 2022)*.

Take, for instance, that you are reading this book. You have discovered your root number is three. Then you calculate the value of your name using the Chaldean techniques and learn your name has a value of 33. These are still coincidental. The numbers have been found purposefully, but they are merely coincidental calculations. Yes, they have a purpose, but they are not necessarily messages from the angels. An hour later, you are walking down your street when you notice a house with the number 33 on it. At this point, you should become more aware of your surroundings, but do not gravitate to the presence of angels yet. Focusing on the number three is plausible, considering you addressed that number in your numerology studies. Now let us say a few hours later, you get a water bill for $330. Then an hour after, the electricity meter reads 33 units left. Your partner comes home at 6:30 while you set a timer on the oven for 30 minutes. Now, the number three has meaning. It was repeated too many times to be coincidental. You have to find the line between what is an everyday occurrence and what is not. This is hard to do. But the rule is, if you see this number three times or more, it means something.

So, what can you do when you believe that angels are messaging you?

Before anything else, analyze your current situation. *Are you at home or out and about? What activities have been occupying your mind?* Write these details down in the corresponding entry in your numerology journal. Then, reflect on a previous time when you encountered the same number. *Where were you then? Have you gone out somewhere or had some other plans for that day?*

This number may occur when you pass a particular street. For whatever reason, that number might be pulling your focus. Perhaps the message the angels are trying to give you has to do with the direction you have been going. Maybe you have been investing your time in a new career path, and they want you to know that you are on the right track. Or possibly they want you to know you are taking a wrong turn and you should stop investing time and effort. There is only one way to know for sure—write the number down and find out what it means. And to gain deeper insight into this number's significance, compare your past experiences with this one.

Number Combinations and Patterns

Number combinations refer to sequences of numbers that appear repeatedly and carry specific meanings in numerology. These combinations may include single-digit numbers, double-digit numbers, or even triple-digit numbers. They can be seen in various aspects of our lives, such as birthdates, phone numbers, addresses, and even license plates.

One of the most common number combinations in numerology is 11:11. It is believed to be a powerful spiritual sign indicating that you are on the right path and in tune with the universe. Other number combinations that are considered significant in numerology include 222, 333, 444, and 555. These combinations are thought to represent different messages and guidance from the divine or spiritual realm.

The meaning of number combinations can also vary based on the individual numbers within the sequence. For instance, the combination of 123 is often associated with creativity, growth, and self-improvement, while the combination of 666 is often associated with negativity or dark energy.

Numerologists believe that number combinations can provide insight into one's life purpose, strengths, and weaknesses. By analyzing the frequency and meaning of number combinations in one's life, a numerologist can offer guidance and advice on how to navigate life's challenges and opportunities.

Overall, number combinations in numerology can be a powerful tool for self-discovery and spiritual growth. They offer a unique perspective on the patterns and energies that govern our lives and can help us better understand our purpose and potential.

Below is a list of all the potential combinations and patterns you may interact with daily. You must learn the affiliated meanings for each so that when you encounter them, you can interpret their meaning and follow through on the right course of action that will land you in happier stead *(5 Powerful Ways, 2022)*.

- ***111***

  This number is associated with God. When you see this number, it means that you are isolating yourself and need to fall back under His hand, the warmth of friends, and the support of loved ones. It reminds you that nothing was built on one sole promise, person, or covenant.

Even God needed the help of Jesus to clear humanity of sin. Jesus needed the guidance and support of His followers to help Him find courage in His journey. God made the angels to assist Him in creating the earth and protecting humankind. Wherever you are and whatever you are doing, you cannot do it alone.

- *222*

When you see the number two, it could remind you to bring balance into your life. Maybe you are allowing yourself too much indulgence and missing out on your true purpose or not giving in enough and prohibiting natural events from taking place. If this number appears, look at your actions and then go in the opposite direction.

- *333*

Having this number appearing in your life over and over can state a solid creative force bubbling within you. Embrace this power and create something meaningful like a book, poem, movie, or song. Transform your imaginative vision into a lasting art form or take that leap of faith and attend the audition you have been pondering.

- *444*

An angel will appear to you with this special number, letting you know they are there for your support and comfort. This number reminds them that they are by your side and will help guide you as needed. They do not want you to feel alone. Furthermore, it is a sign for you to put careful planning into everything you do. For whatever reason, the angels need you to think through your choices. The angels know that if you think through things, you will make the right choice. However, you need to be more careful with your actions.

- *555*

Embrace the new opportunities in front of you when this number appears. Take that walk you have been thinking about, call up someone and ask them to dinner, or head to that gathering at the restaurant. The angels tell you everything will be alright; only good is on the horizon. So, step out of your comfort zone and see what blessings await.

- *666*

Noticing the number six might signify that you are about to experience some loss to yourself or someone you care for. To avoid this, take advantage of this time to surround yourself with friends and family and make the most of it. Gathering those close to you can help provide a good source of comfort and joy.

- *777*

Seeing the number seven means that your angels are very pleased with the decisions you have been making, and they want you to know that you are on the right path. Hence, your destiny lies ahead of you down the path you have been taking. You are in perfect harmony with the universe, and it wants to show you that all is as it should be. Keep making the choices you have been and stay open to what comes your way; all will continue to be right. When the time comes, you will discover your true purpose in life and feel whole, knowing that everything that has happened up until now has true meaning. Everything will continue to make sense and bring you joy along the way.

- *888*

The angels have heard your distress and have sent eight angelic acknowledgments to reaffirm your strength. Lending their love and light, they are showing you the way forward, as some doors will be opened for you, so stay motivated by selecting the right ones. Keep yourself in balance by trusting these divine energies to guide you through times of pain. However, when you repeatedly see this number and do not feel very hopeful, it makes opening the right doors hard. But if you can find the strength to stay positive in times of crisis and know that someone is looking out for you, you will discover those doors quickly, and your pain will be alleviated.

- *999*

Something in your life may end, and this number is a sign of that. It could be the end of a project, a relationship, or even a milestone. Whatever it is, you must acknowledge that something will end and let it. This is the angels' way of asking you to let something go and, at the same time, telling you it will be okay.

- *000*

New beginnings are coming your way when you see this number over and over. It is crucial to remain focused and positive because something unique is about to happen to you. Let it.

- *Triple-digit patterns*

Witnessing numbers repeating in threes signifies that angels are with you and influencing your life. Listen carefully to your thoughts, analyze your dreams, and explore your spiritual gifts because the line to the spirit world is ringing, and someone on the other side wants to talk to you.

Chapter 15:
Angels and Their Messages

From the moment you were set to embark upon your journey here on Earth, God blessed you with the persistent presence of angels. They guided your soul through the passage into your mother's womb and were there as you entered the world. Even today, they remain steadfastly by your side, understanding and knowing you more deeply than perhaps even yourself. You can feel their assurance in the unexplainable yet resonating part of yourself you often forget when trying to make sense of this world. A piece that contains the truth about who you are, what drives you, and where your destiny lies.

But who are the angels exactly? Are we surrounded by multiple angels or just one? How do we know who is watching over us? Will they ever reach out? If they do, how do we interpret this? How do we respond?

Firstly, multiple angels and spiritual beings are watching over each of us. These spirits may be close friends or family members who have passed away, souls we encountered in past lives, or angelic spirits God has asked to watch over us. But we all have one particularly powerful angelic being watching over us and assisting in our journey—an archangel. Archangels play essential roles in our lives. They guide, protect, and support us along our journey. Furthermore, they were created to fulfill specific missions, protect humans against evil, and help God's ultimate plan come to light. There are hundreds of archangels, but only seven are originals, as they were the first archangels created by God: *Michael, Raphael, Gabriel, Jophiel, Ariel, Azrael,* and *Chamuel.*

Finding Your Guardian Angel

Knowing who your specific guardian angel is will help you understand your life's journey. If you know who your guardian angel is, you can talk to them and ask for advice regularly. You can receive angelic messages daily and ensure you are on the path to a happy and fulfilled life. *But how can you find out who your archangel is?*

Finding your guardian angel is as easy as adding up the numbers in your birth date and reducing them to a single-digit number from one to nine. As such, let us see if we can identify Princess Diana's guardian angel. Diana Frances Spencer was born on the 1st of July, 1961 *(Diana, Princess of Wales, n.d.).* Her guardian angel equation is as follows:

$1 + 7 + 1 + 9 + 6 + 1 = 25 = 2 + 5 = 7$

The archangel Raphael is the guardian angel associated with seven, symbolizing comfort and health. Diana embodied all these same qualities that her guardian angel stands for. Meanwhile, when you know who your archangel is, you can seek out its guidance.

The Archangels

Below you will find a list of the archangels and their numbers:

- *Raguel (One)*

  Being associated with number one is all about invention and pioneering. This can be an intimidating force to reckon with. However, those who have Raguel close by can call on him and harness his courage when starting new endeavors. With a name that means "friend of God," he is the embodiment of harmony. He is not just the source of miracles; he can also give you the strength to do anything. Not only does he provide knowledge but also energy for all types of undertakings.

- *Uriel (Two)*

  Uriel is considered a heavenly emissary, a source of solace during hard times. Being associated with him allows one to summon his power and make sound decisions in the face of difficulty. With Uriel by your side, you will always be guided and make wise choices.

- *Jophiel (Three)*

  Like the number three, Jophiel is enthusiastic, creative, and happy. His power can help you create visionary music, art, and plays. He will motivate and inspire you to work hard, overcome obstacles, and complete unfinished work. If you are connected with this angel, you are undoubtedly on a creative mission. And so, Jophiel can enhance your creative abilities when needed.

- ### *Haniel (Four)*

This archangel can bring about significant changes to your character, ideas, relationships, and life. Drawing from his formidable skills in building solid foundations, he is an ideal companion if you aim for stable relationships. He also helps maintain precarious careers and can keep your spirits up even during trying times. You can call on Haniel to fill you with joy and to help those around you find it too. Ergo, if you see messages from this angel, listen—they are trying to make you happier.

- ### *Jeremiel (Five)*

Jeremiel is a confident rebel who is unafraid to tackle the dangerous, the impossible, and the challenging. When you see messages from this angel, know that he is encouraging you to go into battle unafraid. Some battles are destined to happen, some fights are meant to be had, and some losses are meant to be lost. Call on Jeremiel when you need the strength to face your problems. With unyielding kindness and tempered bravery, he will shepherd you toward understanding. He will also provide you with mercy when you cannot bring even an ounce of it to yourself and guide you to justice in any situation.

- ### *Michael (Six)*

This angel is the closest to God, the embodiment of justice, mercy, and righteousness. He strives for peace in all circumstances and does his utmost to prevent violence. When you are afraid, you should call on St. Michael with the following affirmation: *"Help me, help me, help me, St. Michael."* If you say it three times, he will come. You will feel his energy enter the room, and you won't be scared anymore.

- *Raphael (Seven)*

Offering help and understanding, he will give you comfort and guidance. Raphael has an innate knowledge of your body; he knows when it is time to nourish yourself with food, take that much-needed rest, and provide it with extra care. Not only did he witness your heart's initial beat and your lungs' first breath, but he was also aware when something was not quite right. If you see messages from him, know that he is trying to keep you healthy. You might need to go for a checkup at the doctor, eat, or take the day off from work. Strong ties to this angel give you the power to feel your needs better. Call on Raphael when you want to sense your destiny and desires more clearly.

- *Raziel (Eight)*

The angel of mysteries receives messages from God to relay to others. If you are receiving messages from him, know that you have reached a deeper relationship with a higher power and are on the right path toward enlightenment. Your senses may become heightened. You may feel light-headed and be able to understand your reason for existing better. To be connected with Raziel allows you to harness an intuitive power that lets you sense your choices and opportunities more clearly.

- *Ariel (Nine)*

Receiving messages from this angel is a sign that you need to embrace a more peaceful life. Ariel is a beacon of hope within the celestial realm as she helps all living things live in harmony. *Why does the antelope not avenge the lion?* This is because God has sent Ariel to help them coexist. Her role is to ensure that the environment and humanity live harmoniously. Acquiring messages from her could be a sign to protect your environment further, to let go of past frustrations, and to live in peace. You can call on her to tap into her power of greenery and connection. She might be helpful when starting a garden, beginning new projects, and making new friends.

Manifesting with Angels

Once you understand archangels' different properties and associated numbers, you can use them and call on them whenever you need. And you do not need to wait for angels to send you a message before communicating with them, as you can share with them at this very moment. Moreover, everything in the universe vibrates, including our desires. By attaching the number associated with your needs to an angelic number, you can connect with angels and fulfill your deepest desires and needs.

Luck	Happiness	Job	Love	Success
5	2	1	2	1
7	3	3	3	3
9	8	4	6	4
	9		8	

Let us use Princess Kate in this example. Catherine Middleton was born on the 9th of January, 1982 *(Catherine Princess of Wales, n.d.)*. Her guardian angel equation reads as follows:

$$9 + 1 + 1 + 9 + 8 + 2 = 30 = 3 + 0 = 3$$

The archangel associated with Kate Middleton is Jophiel, the angel of new beginnings and creativity. Kate could call on any angel to guide her. Yet, she is likely to get faster answers that will make more sense to her when they have come from the angel who knows her most intimately.

As such, imagine that before meeting Prince William, she prayed to Jophiel for love. One way she could do this is to place Jophiel's number at the beginning and end of her sequence: *3x3*.

Numbers represent the essence of love and connection: *two, three, six, and eight*. Kate can use any of those digits as the center point, from *323, 363, 333,* or *383*, and it will all be accepted just the same. The threes, in particular, symbolize who will answer and receive the call, emphasizing that paramount importance lies within the number right in the middle. Likewise, if she wrote this number sequence multiple times, she could send a message to the angels asking them for guidance in her love life.

However, you do not need to restrict your contact with the archangels to only your own; you can call on any angel you like. You can reach out directly to other angels too. Yet, know that the lines of communication are always strongest when talking to the one that knows you best.

Pillar 6:
Numerological Cycles

Numerological cycles studies the mystical relationship between numbers and events in your life. These cycles refer to the idea that your time here on earth is divided into different periods, each of which is associated with a particular number and has its own unique energy and characteristics. Understanding these cycles can help you make more informed decisions about your future.

The three primary cycles in numerology are personal year cycles, pinnacles, and challenges, each of which is determined by calculations based on your birth date and name.

Chapter 16: The Pinnacles

In numerology, Pinnacles refer to four long-term cycles in your life that represent specific challenges, lessons, and opportunities you might encounter.

The four Pinnacle cycles cover your entire lifespan. Each one begins after the previous one ends, and they are all of different lengths.

The First Pinnacle

First Pinnacle: This cycle begins at birth and lasts until the age of 36 minus your Life Path number.

This pinnacle is associated with the number 1 and represents the start of a new cycle, the beginning of a journey of self-discovery and self-expression.

During this stage, you're likely to experience a sense of newfound independence and confidence. You may feel a strong desire to assert yourself and make your mark on the world. This is a time of exploration and experimentation, as you begin to develop your unique identity and find your purpose.

The energy of the first pinnacle is characterized by initiative, leadership, and individuality. In this stage, you're encouraged to take risks and pursue your passions, even if it means going against the norm or facing criticism from others. This is a time to build a strong foundation for future success, and to cultivate the courage and determination needed to achieve your goals.

The Second Pinnacle

The second cycle starts after the first ends and lasts for 9 years.

During this cycle, you try hard to cooperate, share, and work with others. Relationships take priority in your life, and you strive to form close, supportive bonds while keeping your values intact. Fostering meaningful partnerships is at the top of your list as you endeavor to make connections that matter. No matter what comes your way, your values will remain unscathed. *(Pinnacles and Challenge Numbers, 2017).*

You may also experience a shift in focus and perspective that can lead to significant personal and spiritual growth. This cycle is often associated with career changes, new relationships, and other major life events that can have a lasting impact on your trajectory.

The Third Pinnacle

The third cycle starts after the second cycle ends and also lasts for 9 years. During this cycle, one becomes intimately familiar with one's habits and character. As a result, one will test the boundaries of their knowledge. Self-expression, taxing patience and trying new things are all events one may experience during this course *(Pinnacles and Challenge Numbers, 2017)*.

This is the time of spiritual growth and self-discovery. You may begin to question your beliefs and values, find the need to speak your truths, and seek out new sources of inspiration and guidance. You may also feel drawn to social and humanitarian causes, and may seek out opportunities to make a difference.

The Fourth Pinnacle

The fourth cycle starts after the third cycle ends and continues for the rest of your life. It is associated with hard work, stability, and achievement. It's a time when you're likely to reap the rewards of your previous efforts and may find yourself in a position of authority or leadership. This can be a very productive and fulfilling time, as long as you remain focused and dedicated to your goals.

One of the key themes of the fourth pinnacle is responsibility. This is a time when you're called to take ownership of your actions and decisions, and to be accountable for your impact on others. You will be tested on everything you have learned. To be successful during this cycle, you will need unwavering beliefs, strong friendships, and a stable career. Without these aspects, you will wear yourself thin by doing too much with minimal support *(Pinnacles and Challenge Numbers, 2017)*. So, you must pour in the foundation for your future, manifest the right opportunities, and immerse yourself in supportive, positive, and realistic energies. It would not help to anticipate larger-than-life events coming your way. Think practically and rationally, and do not be hasty.

Understanding what you need to learn will give you a sense of instant gratification. Having an idea of what you should achieve makes reaching that goal far easier and quicker, allowing you to anticipate any roadblocks before they even present themselves. By being aware of the transformation ahead and taking the right steps in preparation, your transition will be effortless, gentle, and stress-free. This way, you will have very few friends lost along the way and readily accept new changes. *Does not that sound comforting?*

Chapter 17:
Numbers and Their Challenges

Each pinnacle period or cycle is associated with a pinnacle number. These numbers represent the specific energy or influence that will dominate during a particular pinnacle cycle of your life.

Each pinnacle number carries a specific vibrational energy that is understood through the numerological meaning of the numbers 1-9, and potentially the master numbers 11, 22, and 33.

Below, you will find a detailed list of the numbers one to nine and their associated meanings concerning the four cycles. In this case, these numbers do not have a universal understanding. Instead, their purposes and intensities are subject to your cycle *(Pinnacles and Challenge Numbers, 2017)*.

- *One*

  The number one concerns finding courage in facing an adversary, learning to stand up for yourself, and becoming self-reliant. This number calls for one to step up and learn fast. With this number in your destiny, you will have to perform and learn simultaneously. As such, you will act like a musician trying to keep up with the -band while still learning to play the instrument. It will be an intense and challenging time, but if you keep your focus and stick to your values, you can avoid being overpowered by those more mature than you. Ergo, your challenge is to find the courage to realize when you are becoming overwhelmed and refocus your energies on your sense of self.

- *Pinnacle One*

  To experience number one in your first pinnacle means you will spend much of your initial development trying to form original ideas and find your identity. You will be called to lead without knowing what you are getting into and without being able to rely on yourself. It will be a challenging time. All eyes will be on you, waiting for you to make a wrong step. Likewise, you will make mistakes because you are learning as you go. Mistakes are inevitable, especially when you do not know what you are doing. Learn to embrace them to avoid looking back on yourself negatively later in life. Remain positive, and do not let your ego get in your way.

- *Pinnacles Two and Three*

  Focusing on your courage, drive, and vision during this cycle will prime you for leadership. Knowing and holding unwaveringly to your values is necessary. Hence, taking on a sterner outlook may be critical. Determination and integrity will also come into play, but only if you can discern your values and strive to keep them.

- *Pinnacle Four*

  With number one as the driving force in your fourth pinnacle, you are not likely to retire soon. Instead, you are destined to work harder than ever and accomplish great things in your leadership positions. You will be challenged to find new creative ways to enhance harmony and independence in your life.

- *Two*

This number encourages partnerships, cooperation, sharing, balance, and patience. You are likely to encounter many teamwork opportunities. Your challenge is to learn how to relate to and understand others while maintaining your values. Furthermore, you will need to find creative ways to compromise comfortably. While this number encourages you to look to others, it does not suggest a parallel. Likewise, you will sense that others cannot be bothered to do for you what you would do for them. This could make you bitter and resentful. Yet, try not to let the behavior of others get you down. Focus on what you can control, who you are, and the good you can do, and then you will be happy.

- *Pinnacle One*

  If you experience the number two within your first pinnacle, you can expect to be overly sensitive, easily hurt, and empathic. You will feel many emotions and not understand what to do with them. And so, your challenge is to make yourself comfortable by inviting others to help you assess these emotions and learn to cope with them.

- *Pinnacles Two and Three*

  During these stages, you will feel the effects of working with others in a balanced and harmonious setting. This wonderful and peaceful experience should encourage you to find ways to enjoy this kind of cooperation more frequently. The work you engage in during this time will be challenging, detailed, and plentiful. Thus, you will need to work well with others to help you get through.

- *Pinnacle Four*

  Having two energies influencing your fourth pinnacle will bring harmony and opportunity. Then, you can retire or continue to work a balanced and fulfilling career. The wonderful news is that you get to choose. However, you will need to watch your growing sensitivity. If you can get your emotions in control, you can live happily and cooperatively with those you care for most.

- *Three*

Number three proposes an opportunity to get to know yourself better. Your challenge is to dig deep and locate your emotions, their causes, and methods you can use to cope with them. This number forecasts your learning to share your feelings openly.

- *Pinnacle One*

  Number three revealing itself during your first pinnacle is a sign that you will have to learn how to navigate a creative path. Likely, you will participate in something requiring creative vision, understanding, and skill. Chances are, you will not have the wisdom or the ability to see your dreams through, but you will have many pleasures in creating them. Focus your energy on creation rather than follow through, lest you become bitter and resentful at a young age.

- *Pinnacles Two and Three*

In the second and third pinnacles, the number three brings good friends, stable relationships, joy, and creative self-expression. With the number three, accomplishments are limited to how well you get along with others. Ever heard the saying, *"It is who you know, not what you know?"* That applies to you now more than ever.

- *Pinnacle Four*

The number three in the fourth pinnacle presents a good chance of travel and social activity rather than hard work.

- *Four*

As number four draws in, it signifies a need for family and stability. Yet, it will be challenging because you are learning to set good foundations, think with caution, and work sequentially. Overall, four encourages you to work hard to enjoy a blissful future.

- *Pinnacle One*

Four in the first pinnacle represents a demanding childhood with economic challenges, hard work, and lots of effort. It is a stage of life where you will be devoted to your education and future career. There is also a little frivolity and lots of stress and high-pressure settings.

- *Pinnacles Two and Three*

  A four in your second and third pinnacles promotes a chance to achieve and get ahead in your industry. You will develop a competitive drive that will propel you toward success. But you must have courage in the foundations you have set, as there will be setbacks.

- *Pinnacle Four*

  The four energies in the fourth stage of life leaves one unlikely to slow down or retire. And while working hard, you will find plenty of joy. Besides that, you will know your limitations and be able to control and balance your career and social life optimally.

- *Five*

This number signifies a call for transformation. As such, it encourages us to open up and explore, allowing us to release our previous limitations. It also represents freedom, liberation, and exciting opportunities. Adapting to our ever-changing environment requires us to be flexible and prepared for the unknown.

- *Pinnacle One*

  Establishing stability and discovering your identity can be tough when the number five comes up during your first life stage. This could cause frequent travel, relationship break-ups, and career changes. You may also get into trouble often, with intense cravings and desires that are hard to resist. Setting beneficial intentions and maintaining healthy limits will help you make sensible choices without taking too much risk.

- *Pinnacles Two and Three*

  The vibrational influence of five brings progress and high achievement in your second and third pinnacles. Your desire for freedom will be quite powerful during this stage, but you must be careful not to let go of too many relationships and friendships.

- *Pinnacle Four*

  A five in the last stage of your life limits your ability to slow down. Instead, you will be in a fast-paced setting, startled by change and variety. You will overreach financially and domestically. To get through, you will have to build resilience. Remember, the mistakes you make do not define you. Errors only form part of your evolution, not the end product.

- *Six*

The number six draws family, relationships, service, and love into one's life. With a six in the works, you will need to find a balance between the amount you receive and the amount you give. Moreover, you will have to learn to pull away when your actions are not reciprocated. Similarly, you will learn to give back when required. Yet, the challenge is fighting your sense of responsibility. Reminding yourself that you are not the answer to everyone's problems is also essential. Hence, you do not have to try and fix their issues, only your own. Likewise, letting go when you are 'drowning' in pressure is okay. Focusing on yourself can also help those around you in the long run.

- *Pinnacle One*

  If you have number six involved in the first stage of your life, you will likely feel much pressure around caring for your family. The challenge is to find ways to remain a child while quickly growing into a mature and concerned adult. Life will deal you rough cards, but you need to remind yourself that none of it is your fault, and you are not responsible for the actions of adults, only your own.

- *Pinnacles Two and Three*

  The vibrations on a six within your second and third pinnacles influence your focus on your family. So, concentrate more on those you care for than your work. Likewise, you will be happiest when developing yourself as an individual.

- *Pinnacle Four*

  A fourth pinnacle, combined with the number six, adds a sense of philanthropy to your existence. Hence, you will find you are happiest in giving rather than receiving.

- *Seven*

Learning and studying are the major influences a seven can bring into your life. Thus, isolating yourself from others as you further your career is natural, but striking a balance between work and social life is a challenge that should be embraced. Working alone may bring the most satisfaction, though finding pleasure in other aspects of life is equally important. That said, you should push yourself to be among others to avoid isolating yourself completely.

- *Pinnacle One*

If you experience a seven in your first few years of life, you will often feel isolated and alone. You may choose to suffer in silence and focus your pain on understanding the meaning behind your life. This will gain you much intellect and intuition, but you will be lonely. Remember to ask for help when you need it. Emotions are normal, so you should not be embarrassed to feel sad. Everyone feels that way sometimes.

- *Pinnacles Two and Three*

The presence of seven within the second and third pinnacles offers a chance to specialize in the spiritual realm. Unless you actively use your intuitive and philosophical skills, progress at this stage can feel taxing, mundane, and slow. Practice your skills readily, and you will find success easily. Aside from that, you will find the most happiness in spiritual and charitable activities during this cycle.

- *Pinnacle Four*

Understanding the depths of knowledge you possess can make it challenging to connect with those around you. So, it is wise to seek out individuals with similar interests and perspectives on life. Likewise, be open and brave, and let others hear your words, as it will help you find like-minded friends. Overall, experiencing the number seven during this pinnacle prepares you to become a spiritual teacher.

- ***Eight***

Power, money, business, and abundance are associated with this number. If you are endowed with an eight, you have been blessed with opportunities to have power, make money, and succeed. Under its influence, you will have to keep control of your judgment, virtues, and sense of right and wrong because you will likely lose yourself and make hasty decisions with so many offerings. Therefore, you need to find the courage to stick to your values.

  - ***Pinnacle One***

  With the number eight associated with your first few years of life, you will become interested in business activity. You can help your family run their business or start your own. Your focus and drive in creating and running a business will be unyielding. But at such a young age, you will likely fumble over many obstacles. However, with patience and grace, you will become satisfied and energized.

  - ***Pinnacles Two and Three***

  The number eight within these life periods invites a more rational way of thinking. Subsequently, you will have to limit your emotions and try to think as often as possible. Meanwhile, your focus will be on your ambitions and achievements. With a clear head and straight values, you can gain much honorable success and power.

  - ***Pinnacle Four***

  In your last stage of life, eight pulls you to develop your wealth and power further. Likewise, giving back your knowledge and passion to others will make you feel best. However, you will have to ration with your years of success to give back and find happiness. Thinking charitably will be difficult at first, but it will help you gain a long-lasting legacy in the long run.

- *Nine*

Number nine promotes the development of a true humanitarian. It allows you to develop charitable attributes like compassion, love, ethics, and patience. Whenever you go, strive to spread encouragement and wisdom and foster peace. Meanwhile, nine can also lead to intense moments of vulnerability when desperately trying to voice your feelings. Through it, remember the power of maintaining emotional balance. Furthermore, you must commit to the concept of the right place and right time when it comes to personal feelings and questions.

- *Pinnacle One*

A child with the number nine influencing their life is a silent hero on the path of everyday life. They stand up for those who are bullied, do not fear retribution, and do what their hearts and teachers have taught them is right and just.

- *Pinnacles Two and Three*

The vibrational pattern of the number nine in these pinnacles pulls forth emotional expression and humanitarian views. You will be happiest doing charitable work, fighting for change, and engaging in political action. Hence, your purpose is to effect change and promote compassion.

- *Pinnacle Four*

  Having nine in your fourth pinnacle favors charity above all else. Consequently, you will be given many opportunities to give of yourself. Likewise, you may retire or invest time in helping others find harmony and balance.

- *Master Number 11*

This number represents the intuitive visionary. It is associated with spiritual insight, enlightenment, and a strong connection with the subconscious mind. With this influence, you may find yourself drawn to seek a deeper understanding of the world around you and the spiritual realms.

- *Pinnacle One*

  A person with Master number 11 influencing their first Pinnacle is likely to experience a heightened sense of intuition and spiritual awareness early in life. This can lead to a strong desire for self-discovery and a fascination with the metaphysical world. They may find themselves naturally drawn to situations that require insight, empathy, and understanding.

- *Pinnacles Two and Three*

  During these Pinnacles, the vibrational energy of the Master number 11 may lead to a deepening of spiritual understanding and the development of psychic abilities. There may also be an increased interest in humanitarian causes, and a desire to contribute to the greater good. These are periods for introspection, growth, and personal transformation.

- *Pinnacle Four*

  Having 11 in the fourth Pinnacle suggests a time of spiritual enlightenment and profound insights. This period may bring opportunities for leadership roles in spiritual or humanitarian fields. The challenges faced during this period will test the person's faith and inner strength, pushing them towards their highest potential.

- *Master Number 22*

This number is known as the Master Builder. It represents practical idealism and the power to turn dreams into reality.

- *Pinnacle One*

  A person influenced by the Master number 22 in their first Pinnacle is likely to demonstrate a unique blend of intuition and practicality. They may exhibit remarkable potential for leadership and a strong ability to manifest their dreams into reality from an early age.

- *Pinnacles Two and Three*

  During these Pinnacles, the vibrational pattern of the Master number 22 can result in a period of considerable productivity and the achievement of significant life goals. There may be opportunities to lead and inspire others and to make a lasting impact on a large scale.

- *Pinnacle Four*

  Having 22 in the fourth Pinnacle suggests a time of significant achievement and the realization of long-term goals.

This is a period of life where the person's leadership skills and ability to manifest will be at its peak, potentially bringing great success and fulfillment.

- *Master Number 33*

This number, known as the Master Teacher, symbolizes selfless service, love, and the spiritual uplifting of mankind.

  - *Pinnacle One*

  A person influenced by the Master number 33 in their first Pinnacle is likely to show a strong tendency towards selflessness and a desire to serve from an early age. They may demonstrate an unusual level of maturity and a deep concern for others.

  - *Pinnacles Two and Three*

  During these Pinnacles, the vibrational pattern of the Master number 33 might lead to a deepening of compassion and a desire to help others. There may be opportunities for teaching, healing, and service, and these are periods for profound personal and spiritual growth.

  - *Pinnacle Four*

  Having 33 in the fourth Pinnacle suggests a time of great spiritual understanding and the potential to make a significant impact on the lives of others. This is a period when the person's capacity for love, healing, and teaching will be at its highest.

How to Calculate

To be able to map out your Pinnacle chart, you need to calculate three general things. They are your:

1. Life path number
2. Pinnacle numbers
3. Pinnacle cycle periods

Let's use the birthdate of Martin Luther King Jr., a well-known civil rights leader, as an example. He was born on January 15, 1929.

1. **Calculate the life path number:** You calculate the life path number by reducing the numbers of the birth date to a single digit or master number (11, 22, 33). Here it would be 1 (Jan) + 15 (day) + 1929 (year) = 1945, then 1+9+4+5 = 19, and finally 1+9 = 10, then 1+0 = 1. Thus, the Life Path number is 1.
2. **Calculate the pinnacle numbers:** Your pinnacle numbers are derived from calculations based on your birth date.
    - First Pinnacle: Add the day and month of birth and reduce to a single digit or master number. For instance, using the above date, 1 (Jan) + 15 = 16, then 1+6 = 7. So, the first Pinnacle number is 7.
    - Second Pinnacle: Add the day of birth and the year of birth and reduce to a single digit or master number. In this case, 15 (day) + 1929 (year) = 1944, then 1+9+4+4 = 18, then 1+8 = 9. So, the second Pinnacle number is 9.
    - Third Pinnacle: Add the first and second Pinnacle numbers and reduce to a single digit or master number. For this ex-

ample, 7 (first Pinnacle) + 9 (second Pinnacle) = 16, then 1+6 = 7. So, the third Pinnacle number is 7.

- Fourth Pinnacle: Add the month and year of birth and reduce to a single digit or master number. For this case, 1 (Jan) + 1929 = 1930, then 1+9+3+0 = 13, then 1+3 = 4. So, the fourth Pinnacle number is 4.

4. **Calculate the pinnacle cycle periods:** The Pinnacle cycles have different durations and are determined by subtracting the Life Path number from 36.

   - First Pinnacle: This cycle starts from birth and continues until the day before your 36th birthday, minus the Life Path Number. In this example, it would be 36 - 1 = 35 years.
   - Second Pinnacle: This cycle starts from your 36th birthday, minus the Life Path Number, and lasts 9 years. In this example, it starts from age 35 and continues until age 44.
   - Third Pinnacle: This cycle starts after the second Pinnacle and also lasts 9 years. So, in this case, it begins at age 44 and goes on until age 53.
   - Fourth Pinnacle: This cycle starts after the third Pinnacle and lasts for the rest of your life. In this case, it starts from age 53 onwards.

Martin Luther King Jr.'s Pinnacle numbers are 7, 9, 7, and 4, and these cycles span from birth to age 35, 35 to 44, 44 to 53, and 53 onwards, respectively. It's interesting to look at the meanings of these numbers and how they might correlate with the major phases of his life.

It is so important to understand the value of calculating the four pinnacles. Doing so allows you to understand what you went through, why your experiences were what they were, and how you can move on without regret.

Here's a general chart showing the different Pinnacle periods based on the Life Path number. Use this to map your own chart. Remember, the age ranges for each pinnacle cycle are calculated by subtracting the life path number from 36.

Life Path Number	1st Pinnacle (Birth - X)	2nd Pinnacle (X - Y)	3rd Pinnacle (Y - Z)	4th Pinnacle (Z onwards)
1	Birth - 35	35 - 44	44 - 53	53 onwards
2	Birth - 34	34 - 43	43 - 52	52 onwards
3	Birth - 33	33 - 42	42 - 51	51 onwards
4	Birth - 32	32 - 41	41 - 50	50 onwards
5	Birth - 31	31 - 40	40 - 49	49 onwards
6	Birth - 30	30 - 39	39 - 48	48 onwards
7	Birth - 29	29 - 38	38 - 47	47 onwards
8	Birth - 28	28 - 37	37 - 46	46 onwards
9	Birth - 27	27 - 36	36 - 45	45 onwards

If your life path number is a master number (11, 22, and 33), reduce them to a single digit (2, 4, and 6 respectively) for the purposes of determining the pinnacle periods. However, you should still consider the Master number interpretations when evaluating your Pinnacle numbers.

Pillar 7:
Year Planning

Calculating what you are supposed to learn in each period of your life is helpful if you are trying to understand what it is you need to achieve and when you need to achieve it. Once you know this, you can learn major life lessons and enjoy a fulfilled and exciting life. Likewise, along the way, you are going to experience many challenges. And likely, you will have many questions about these challenges, such as when they will happen and what you can do to resolve them quickly. Fortunately, numerology has the potential to provide exceptional detail.

Have you ever wondered what the year has in store for you? Have you thought of when you will finally achieve that promotion? Have you been praying to meet the love of your life? Are you begging to know when you will quit your horrible job?

Numerology can give you the answers to all these questions. It can provide detailed accounts of what to expect throughout your year. You can use these details to guide your decision-making and planning.

Chapter 18: Personal Year Numbers

Is this even possible? Can you predict the events of the upcoming year? Has your life been predetermined to a greater extent than you initially thought? Calculating your personal year numbers may help you do that.

Personal year numbers refer to the yearly cycle that an individual goes through. It is calculated by adding the numerology of the current year with the numerology of the individual's birth month and day.

It is said to influence one's experiences and opportunities throughout the year. It can help give you an idea on what to expect during the year and guide your decisions and actions accordingly.

For example, if your personal year number is 5, it may indicate a year of change, adventure, and growth. Understanding personal year numbers can be a helpful tool in gaining self-awareness and making the most of each year.

Let's say someone was born on May 15, 1990, and they want to calculate their personal year number for the year 2023. Here's how they would do it:

First, they would reduce the month and day of their birth to a single digit. May is the fifth month, so 5. The 15th day reduces to 1 + 5 = 6.

5 + 6 = 11, which is a master number, so it is not reduced further.

Next, they would reduce the year they want to calculate to a single digit: 2 + 0 + 2 + 3 = 7.

Finally, they would add their birth number to the current year number: 11 + 7 = 18.

If the resulting number is a double digit, it is reduced to a single digit by adding the two digits together: 1 + 8 = 9.

So for someone born on May 15, 1990, their personal year number for 2023 would be 9.

Chapter 19: Universal Numbers

Another way that you can glimpse of what the future holds is by calculating your universal number. A universal number is a means of predicting what the world can expect in future years. It's derived from the date of birth, by adding the digits of the birthdate and reducing them to a single digit. Each universal number has its unique characteristics that you can feel throughout your lifetime, most especially during major life events. By understanding the characteristics of each number, you'll be able to play to your strengths, make more informed choices, and achieve your goals more effectively.

Numbers and Meanings

Universal numbers range from 1 to 9, with each number holding its own vibrational energy. Below you will find a list of numbers and their associated meanings concerning universal numbers. These meanings can help you know what to expect in future years *(Universal Year Numbers, 2022).*

- *One*

This number suggests the start of new things, new beginnings, and foundations. The general theme is confidence. A year with this number requires you to have the courage to step up to the plate, take the initiative, and follow your dreams. You must also acknowledge that only your fear is holding you back. Ergo, be optimistic and have faith in your future, now more than ever.

If you have goals, now is the time to work toward achieving them. Do not hold back. Likewise, while chasing your dreams, ensure your responsibilities have been taken care of to avoid getting sucked into your new project. You must act with a hint of caution. Think through your decisions carefully, and do not be too hasty.

Moreover, it is an exciting time, but be wary of taking risks. You must be cautious of doing too much. This may lead you to exhaustion. You should pick one project and stick to it until it is finished, then move on to the next. Be sure to separate your time evenly. Also, do your best to live a balanced life filled with friends and worthwhile work. Finally, your energy this year will likely attract red and mineral ruby.

- *Two*

The number two favors relationships, feelings, compassion, and partnerships. A year with the number two suggests preparing for teamwork and group settings. You will find working with others will bring you much happiness. You will have better results in terms of achieving your goals if you communicate and work cooperatively with others.

This year, your energy will attract the colors white and light blue and the minerals moonstone and pearl.

- *Three*

A year influenced by the number three is likely to hold potential for a creative flood, initiative, and imagination. Enjoyment and creativity are the main themes for this number. You will have many opportunities to have fun. However, your responsibilities will likely fall out of reach, allowing you the space to make new friends and develop stable relationships. Push yourself to be more expressive and sociable. Talk about your feelings and open your heart up to those around you.

Your energy this year will attract the color yellow and the mineral topaz.

- *Four*

This number suggests a year of hard work, little frivolity, and much self-improvement. There will be endless opportunities to expand your career.

Four is calling you to make commitments to your work and personal life. This year is all about putting in the effort.

Tackle things slowly and avoid impulsive decisions at all costs. This is a great time for you to practice and master various skills. Set up a neat calendar and make time to improve your career and friendships

This year your energy will attract the color green and minerals emerald and jade.

- *Five*

Such a number suggests uncertainty, change, and freedom. This is a time of transformation and bountiful opportunities are waiting to spring at you. Look closely at your choices and apply the right amount of consideration to all your options.

You must think big and more creatively. Find a solution that will solve four or five central problems instead of searching for multiple fixes. Be adaptable and embrace new experiences and you'll find this time of change in your life as an adventure. Your energy will attract the color blue and the mineral aquamarine.

- *Six*

This number suggests that home relationships and family duties should be the primary focus this year. Now is the time to make adjustments in your home life. You are allowed to change duties in your home and family relationships. You can also find joy within them again. This is a good time to bring closure to your partnerships and stability to your financial troubles and to ask for advice from loved ones.

The challenge is keeping promises to ensure your home's stability. You must be disciplined, loyal, and dedicated to making changes. It would not be easy, but you will have to endure it for the security of your family. Furthermore, take the year to work on your empathy and compassion. Hence, allow yourself to understand and work better with those you care for most.

Likely, your energy this year will attract the color purple and the mineral sapphire.

- *Seven*

The seven bring forth spiritual ideas, meditation, and inner peace. That said, it is a great time to focus on yourself, your patience, your sense of self-worth, and your empathy. Likewise, ask spiritual questions and search for answers. Other than that, take things slowly, make decisions cautiously, meditate, and learn to go with the flow. You may feel the need to take control, but try to resist; learn how to follow others and act as a team player. Let yourself be emotional, creative, and happy.

This year, you can expect your intuition to enhance. As a result, your relationships and social life will improve. So, you should try to relax this year and let your gut guide you toward success. You may not have all the answers, but be confident that you have enough experience to know what paths to take. Now is a great time to remind yourself of how amazing you are. By learning to believe in yourself, you will find your career and relationships work out better.

Your energy will attract the color violet this year and the mineral amethyst.

- *Eight*

An eight symbolizes a year of praise, rewards, and great success. This year you will be flooded with career, material, and financial achievements. As the year brings you abundance, it is the time to focus on your professional goals. It is also a good time to start building your investments.

Meanwhile, you will desire control above all else and become skeptical of life's pleasures. If you let mistrust rule you, your well-being will be affected. So, you have to stay levelheaded and tackle each task as they come. Let go of people who do not support you. They are not worth fighting for right now. You and what you have worked for are worth your energy and focus. That said, do not purposefully burn out any relationships. Let those who have supported you for years help and appreciate you when you need it most. You will need them to make your achievements feel worthwhile.

This year, your color is brown, and your mineral is a diamond.

- *Nine*

This number often signifies a period of giving back and making a positive impact on the world. You may have strong feelings of empathy and compassion for the less fortunate, those who suffer or those in need.

This is the year to focus less on yourself and more on helping others. Volunteer your time, talent, or treasures for causes that you believe in.

Your color this year is white, and your minerals are opal and gold.

Conclusion

Numerology was developed over many years to appeal to and predict the lives of people of all backgrounds and cultures. Its long history in the hands of Romans, Greeks, Israelites, scientists, and religious leaders has accumulated masses of cultural and philosophical value in the art, which can be enjoyed, understood, and respected by people globally today. Even skeptics will find the ideologies around numerology interesting even if they do not believe it can predict anything.

Aside from its rich history, numerology is fun to practice. There is something so soothing about sitting down with a piece of paper and solving a complex equation. Numerology is a rewarding practice because it forces us to use those spaces in our minds that not everybody uses and because the calculations themselves can be challenging. But the real puller is when we come across a value that intrinsically outlines our personality, character, or fault.

Furthermore, numerology helps people in making safe and worthwhile decisions. Even if numerology does not help immediately or provide you with a complete understanding of your experiences, in the long run, it does. Likewise, numerology helped me know where I wanted to go with my life. It gave me alternative options for career paths. In a way, numerology acted like a career counselor, except cheaper and more knowledgeable about my character. It gave me ideas, which gave me hope.

Perhaps, numerology makes you think. Maybe your calculations suggest that you struggle with something but you do not believe you do, or your associated number means you prefer to be alone when you are happiest around other people. Regardless, the next time you hear a friend does not want to be around others, you might understand why. You will also begin to understand your choices better. Likewise, you do not need to pinpoint that understanding to a value you found in this book.

Likely, numerology may have helped you open up to more possibilities and reason with your behavior and attitude, or it might help you accept who you are. Nevertheless, it can help in many ways without giving hard, accurate facts. Plus, it allows us to imagine and see potential in our lives. For such, *how often have you sat back and wished you could dream like a kid again?* Fortunately, numerology gives you that chance. However, it does not happen overnight. Regardless, somewhere along the line, you will find yourself different from the person you once were, except with little accreditations to this book and the study of numerology.

This book has delved into Pythagorean, Chaldean, and Kabbalah approaches to numerology. Although these practices are inherently different and not, one can give you an accurate reading on their own; collectively, the game changes. If you want to develop a detailed reading of yourself or someone else, you should use all three and explore the fundamental questions and calculations of each. Your root number is just as valuable as your matching Kabbalah energies. The Chaldean rearranged birth number is as pivotal in understanding your destiny as your Pythagorean birth number. Your understanding of yourself within these subcategories is as valuable as collective descriptions of you. These tests will collectively give you a deep, complex, and profound characterization of yourself, your life, and your destiny.

People are not one-dimensional pictures. We are not this or that. We are not always doing things, and we are not doing something. We are made up of multiple layers from many experiences. Our understanding of ourselves has to match that. When reading and calculating your destiny and character, you need to use many techniques. Only then can you truly understand how rare and complex you are.

We have discussed the importance of Karma and finding balance within the universe. Whether Karma is just or unjust is beside the point. It is natural and inevitable.

Have you ever heard the tale of the Mpondo king? The Mpondos was a clan in Africa during the 18th century when Shaka Zulu, king of the Zulu people, was conquering all the lands (*King Faku ka Ngqungqushe*, 2022). There were many battles fought over power. Lives were lost, tricks played, foes destroyed, and friends brought to a bloody end. It was an intense time. The Mpondo king knew that if he tried to defeat Shaka Zulu and his band of fierce warriors, the Mpondo kingdom would be lost forever. The Mpondo king was thoughtful, always thinking and never acting. The favoring of thought over action was something his people frowned upon. They wanted him to act as bravely as Shaka. They wanted their kingdom to take over Africa. They did not want a king who thought and thought and thought. But that was who the Mpondo king was. He thought, and after thinking, he would think some more. The cycle continued until he had found an answer he could cherish. He decided he had to allow Shaka Zulu to pass through his kingdom to fight battles on the other side. However, he did not choose to befriend the king but to assist him.

The other clans witnessed this alliance and became angry. They asked the Mpondo king for the same assistance given to Shaka. The Mpondo king thought some more before turning to Shaka and explaining that he shall not pick sides but allow his kingdom to be marched through by all clans expecting to fight battles on the other side. Although the Mpondo kingdom was not lost, it became dense with travelers, vengeful men, and hungry warriors. As the indigenous clans marched through, many locals were injured, attacked, and humiliated. The locals were very cross and began to abandon their king, moving in with more powerful clans that could protect them better. Still, the Mpondo king chose to let peace thrive in his lands instead of violence. Years passed, and the Mpondo king's wife finally gave him a son.

As the years went by, the Mpondo kingdom lost much of its regard. The Mpondo prince watched the warriors as they passed. He had a keen eye for detail and an even greater skill for fighting. The Mpondo prince quickly grew into the greatest warrior Africa had ever seen. His destiny was to become the warrior that would kill Shaka Zulu and restore the Mpondo kingdom to even greater regard.

Do you think this is interesting? I love this story because it shows how miraculous this world is. Stories like this should not be real, but some are, and Karma is undoubtedly as real as any story.

The miraculousness of tales like this makes one wonder if there exists a higher being that watches over us all. Angels are everywhere. They exist to help us on our path toward God's plan. You can communicate with them. You do not need to wait for them to call you. Just write out the relevant numbers and see what happens. Let the activity of speaking to angels bring you peace of mind, even if it is only when you are afraid. Let the angels help you.

While talking with angels, you can start planning the rest of your life. You know now how to calculate the approximate dates of particular events. You know how to calculate when your character will begin to evolve. Now you can plan and ask for help when you need it most. If your pinnacle charts are not detailed enough, phrase specific questions and find when exactly certain events will happen. You can find out when you will get married, meet the love of your life, have your first child, and when your life may end. You can determine these things in approximations, and your calculation may be unexplainably accurate if you are lucky.

Remember, some things are meant to be. Your life path was constructed before your birth. You have a destiny you need to reach. But you also have some free will, and how you get to where you need to go is up to you. Perhaps you have been going through life unguided. Maybe you have been unsure where you are supposed to be and when you are supposed to be there. You do not need to be uncertain anymore. You now can find the inevitable and can distinguish destiny from choice. You have a superpower that you can use quickly and effectively. Use this power, teach it, and practice it as often as you desire. Your happiness is now in your hands, as it was in Moses', , Adam's, and Archimenes,' who were once Perses.

Glossary

Birth number: This number reveals your talents and potential, the pieces of you that you will need to reach your destiny.

Chaldea: A kingdom that existed in what is now Iraq within ancient Southern Babylonian society around 940 B.C.E.

Character number: This number represents the first trait people notice about you, how they perceive you, and how they will interact with you.

Expectancy number: This number symbolizes who you are to others and what others expect from you.

Expression number: This number symbolizes your talents, strengths, and powers.

First impression number: This number determines how you view yourself and your goals.

Guardian angels: Divine messengers sent by God to help us in our life's journey.

Kabbalah: This is an ancient Hebrew knowledge and lifestyle.

Karma: A cosmic system of judgment that bestows punishment and reward on every living creature.

Karmic debt: The punishments we are exposed to as a result of our negative actions toward others.

Master number: Powerful double-digit numbers that guide your understanding of reality.

Numerology: The study of numbers and how they cosmically relate to people and their past, present, and future.

Personal year number: This number can help determine what is in store for you during a particular year.

Pillar: A foundation of knowledge.

Pinnacles: These are cycles that are time frames within one's life where one evolves in different areas.

Pythagoras: A Greek mathematician, astronomer, and philosopher.

Root number: Your root number reveals your true life path, ultimate destiny, and inner character.

Soul number: This number reveals your heart's greatest desires, the things you have always wanted, and the path that will lead you to your ultimate happiness.

Universal number: This number can be used to predict what can be expected within a specific year.

References

Abbot, R. (2021, June 19). Origin stories: Numerology. *Isbourne.* https://www.isbourne.org/blog/origin-of-numerology-isbourne-wellbeing-centre-cheltenham

Adele biography. (n.d.). The Famous People. https://www.thefamouspeople.com/profiles/adele-6088.php

Albert Einstein biography. (n.d.). Vendantu. https://www.vedantu.com/biography/albert-einstein-biography

Albert Einstein net worth. (n.d.). Celebrity Net Worth. https://www.celebritynetworth.com/richest-businessmen/richest-designers/albert-einstein-net-worth/

Amy Jade Winehouse biography. (n.d.). The Famous People. https://www.thefamouspeople.com/profiles/amy-jade-winehouse-691.php

Believe. (2021, May 18). *Karma debt.* Arcbali. https://arcbali.com/en/numerology-concept-of-karmic-debt-cause-and-effect/

Biography of Vincent van Gogh. (2009). Vincent van Gogh. https://www.vincentvangogh.org/biography.jsp

Blakeley, S. (2022, April 9). *Pythagoras biography and accomplishments.* Study. https://study.com/learn/lesson/pythagoras-history-facts.html

Buchanan, M. (2013). *The numerology guidebook: Uncover your destiny and the blueprint of your life.* Hay House, Inc.

Catherine Princess of Wales. (n.d.). Biography. https://www.biography.com/royalty/kate-middleton

Chaldea Al Fusaic. (2022). Al Fusaic. https://www.alfusaic.net/civilizations-101/chaldea

Chaldean numerology vs Pythagorean numerology. (2011, April 14). Astronlogia. https://astronlogia.com/numerology/chaldean-numerology-vs-pythagorean-numerology/

Chinese alphabet. (2019). My Languages. https://mylanguages.org/chinese_alphabet.php

Clevinger, N. (2021, November 14). *One and only: How did Adele get famous?* The Sun. https://www.thesun.co.uk/tvandshowbiz/celebrities/16734901/how-did-adele-get-famous-one-night-only/

Delhi, R. (2020, August 30). *Is numerology a science or a myth.* Raag Delhi. https://www.raagdelhi.com/numerology-science-or-myth/

Diana, Princess of Wales. (n.d.). Royal. https://www.royal.uk/diana-princess-wales

Drayer, R. (2003). *Numerology: The power in numbers.* Square One Publishers, Inc.

Ellen DeGeneres biography. (n.d.). Notable biographies. https://www.notablebiographies.com/news/Ca-Ge/DeGeneres-Ellen.html

Everything about Chaldean numerology. (n.d.). Sylbu. https://slybu.com/chaldean-numerology/

Field, S. (2020). *May 2020 weather history of Indiana.* Weather Spark. https://weatherspark.com/h/m/19729/2020/5/Historical-Weather-in-May-2020-in-Indiana-Pennsylvania-United-States

5 powerful ways to manifest with angel numbers (rituals). (2022, May 14). Manifest Like Whoa. https://manifestlikewhoa.com/manifest-with-angel-numbers

Gomez, J. (2022, 24th August). *Aileen Wuornos.* Metro Biography. https://metrobiography.com/aileen-wuornos/

Haim, J. (2018, August 3). *The energy centers of Kabbalah.* Wellbeing. https://www.wellbeing.com.au/mind-spirit/spirituality/energy-centres-kabbalah.html

Handel biography—History of George Frideric Handel. (2018, April 17). C Muse. https://www.cmuse.org/handel-biography-george-frideric-handel-composer-history/

The history of numerology. (2022). Numerology Toolbox. https://numerologytoolbox.com/numerology/history-of-numerology/

How to predict timing of events. (2022). Affinity Numerology. https://affinitynumerology.com/using-numerology/predict-timing-of-events.php#maincontentcontinue

Hungarian alphabet. (2019). My Languages. https://mylanguages.org/hungarian_alphabet.php

Jeffrey Dahmer biography. (2022, September 26). Biography. https://www.biography.com/crime-figure/jeffrey-dahmer

Jin, H., and Oguh, C. (2022, October 28). *Explainer: How Elon Musk funded the $44 billion Twitter deal.* Reuters. https://www.reuters.com/markets/us/how-will-elon-musk-pay-twitter-2022-10-07

Joanna, E. (2022, March 23). *Pythagoras: Life, work, and achievements.* Live Science. https://www.livescience.com/pythagoras

Kabbalah numerology. (2022). My Pandit. https://www.mypandit.com/numerology/types/kabbalah/#kabbalah-numerology-reading

Kabbalah numerology: Meanings with numbers and reading chart. (n.d.). Slybu. https://slybu.com/kabbalah-numerology/

Karmic numbers. (2020). Numerology Savvy. https://numerologysavvy.com/karmic-numbers/

King Faku ka Ngqungqushe. (2022, June 29). SA History. https://www.sahistory.org.za/people/king-faku-ka-ngqungqushe

Learn languages. (2019). My Languages. https://mylanguages.org/

Let numerology answer your question. (2022). Truthstar. https://www.truthstar.com/let-numerology-answer-your-question/

Lock, S. (2020, September 11). *When did the Twin Towers fall and what does the World Trade Center look like now?* The Sun. https://www.the-sun.com/news/1455693/when-twin-towers-fall-world-trade-center-9-11-terror-attack/

Lopez, C. (2021, June 20). *Ted Bundy: Biography of a serial killer.* Warbleton Council. https://warbletoncouncil.org/ted-bundy-7767

McKoy, J. (2021, October 7). *Depression rates in US tripled when the pandemic first hit—Now, they're even worse.* The Brink. https://www.bu.edu/articles/2021/depression-rates-tripled-when-pandemic-first-hit

Michelle Obama biography. (2018, February 26). Biography. https://www.biography.com/us-first-lady/michelle-obama

Nathan, S. (2022, May 14). *Ellen DeGeneres preps for her TV farewell: She's 'been crying a lot'.* Page six. https://pagesix.com/2022/05/14/ellen-degeneres-preps-for-last-show-shes-been-crying

Nina Simone. (n.d.). Ninasimone.com. https://www.ninasimone.com/biography/

Number meanings 1–9. (2022). Numerology. https://www.numerology.com/articles/about-numerology/single-digit-numbers-in-numerology/

Numerology—The meaning of natural numbers. (2022). Number Academy. https://number.academy/numerology/

Olivia. (2022). *Everything you need to know about Chaldean numerology.* Just Numerology. https://justnumerology.com/chaldean-numerology

Pinnacles and challenge numbers. (2017, March 17). Felicia Bender. https://feliciabender.com/pinnacles-and-challenge-numbers

Queen Elizabeth II. (2022, September 26). Biography. https://www.biography.com/royalty/queen-elizabeth-ii

Reed, L. (2020). *What are master numbers and what do they mean.* Simply New Age. https://simplynewage.com/what-are-master-numbers-and-what-do-they-mean

Richard. (2020, May 2). *Numerology calculation—The Pythagorean method.* Character Numerology. https://characternumerology.com/numerology-calculation-the-pythagorean-method/

Selene. (2022, August 4). *Using manifestation numbers.* Psychicsource. https://www.psychicsource.com/article/other-psychic-topics/manifesting-with-numbers-by-psychic-selene/24104

Slick, M. (2008, December 5). *The origins and history of Kabbalah.* Carm. https://www.carm.org/kabbalah/the-origins-and-history-of-kabbalah/

Taylor Swift biography. (n.d.). Famous People. https://www.thefamouspeople.com/profiles/taylor-swift-13896.php

The surprising ways that Chaldean numerology will unlock your destiny! (2022). Numerologist. https://numerologist.com/numerology/4-things-you-need-to-know-about-chaldean-numerology/#chaldean11

Universal year numbers—What they are and how to calculate them! (2022). Numerologist. https://numerologist.com/numerology/universal-year-number-calculate

Wang, J. (2022, September 16). *What is the average net worth by age in America?* Best Wallet Hacks. https://wallethacks.com/average-net-worth-by-age-americans/

What is Kabbalah. (2022). The Kabbalah Center. https://www.kabbalah.com/en/pages/what-is-kabbalah/

Zulu alphabet. (2019). My Languages. https://mylanguages.org/zulu_alphabet.php

Made in the USA
Coppell, TX
14 January 2024